W9-AVK-575

THE FEMME FATALE
IN AMERICAN LITERATURE

THE FEMME FATALE IN AMERICAN LITERATURE

Ghada Suleiman Sasa

CAMBRIA
PRESS

AMHERST, NEW YORK

Requests for permission should be directed to:
permissions@cambriapress.com, or mailed to:
Cambria Press
20 Northpointe Parkway, Suite 188
Amherst, NY 14228

Library of Congress Cataloging-in-Publication Data

Sasa, Ghada.
    The femme fatale in American literature / Ghada Sasa.
        p. cm.
    Includes bibliographical references and index.
    ISBN 978-1-60497-535-2 (alk. paper)
    1. American fiction—19th century—History and criticism. 2. Women in literature. 3. Women and literature—United States—History—19th century. 4. Sex role in literature. 5. Naturalism in literature. 6. Dreiser, Theodore, 1871–1945. Sister Carrie. 7. Norris, Frank, 1870–1902. McTeague. 8. Chopin, Kate, 1851–1904. Awakening. 9. Larsen, Nella. Quicksand. I. Title.

    PS374.W6S27 2008
    813'.309—dc22

2008019295

To my dear and loving family:
To Muhammad, Noor, Yousef, and Sara,
I love you with all my heart.

TABLE OF CONTENTS

FOREWORD

The femme fatale is a standard archetype in American literature. The enchantress, the siren, the dangerous man-trap, has been a feature of American fiction from the outset. James Fenimore Cooper and Nathaniel Hawthorne both employ alluring dark-haired ladies, often as foils for their innocent blondes, to captivate their heroes and distract them from their manly pursuits: women like Cooper's Cora Munro and Hawthorne's Hester, Zenobia, and Miriam. Similar seductive females populate the works of modern and postmodern writers: F. Scott Fitzgerald's Daisy Buchanan enchants and eventually causes the downfall of Jay Gatsby, Vladimir Nabokov's Lolita mesmerizes Humbert Humbert, and Lennie falls victim to Curly's wife in John Steinbeck's *Of Mice and Men*. Little has been written, however, about the role of the femme fatale in the fiction of the naturalistic writers of the late nineteenth and early twentieth centuries, perhaps because the seductive power of the femme fatale implies much greater agency than the naturalistic writers' vision would permit. However, that gap in scholarship has now been filled by Ghada Suleiman Sasa's insightful *The Femme Fatale in American Literature*, an exploration of the subtle and complex role of the femme fatale in writers like Frank Norris, Kate Chopin, Theodore Dreiser, and Nella Larsen. Sasa positions these naturalistic femmes fatales between the more powerful femmes fatales of both the romantic period and the modern period. Sasa points out that most critics of naturalistic fiction portray women characters as little more than weak and passive pawns, stereotyped victims of either men or forces of fate, heredity, and environment. However, Sasa argues that, despite the deterministic mood and the social and economic limitations imposed upon heroines of naturalistic fiction, numerous women manage, at least temporarily, to resist and rise above these limitations and, by their powers of enchantment, to defeat heredity and environment.

Sasa, thus, discovers a duality in the femme fatale of much naturalistic fiction. On one hand, Sasa's femme fatale is "strong, daring, and determined." She exploits her sexuality in order to escape the forces of heredity and environment that constrain her. In the process she becomes a victimizer who possesses the power to bend men to her will and accomplish her own selfish goals. On the other hand, the femme fatale of American naturalism is fated for failure, disillusionment, even death. Despite her initial successes, she ultimately falls victim to forces of society and fate over which she has little control.

The complex view of the femme fatale in *The Femme Fatale in American Literature* is compelling because it reinforces one of the most consistent theories of critics who have written extensively about essential characteristics of naturalistic authors and their texts. Various literary critics mention the presence of an element of tension in traditional texts of American naturalism, an element that is not necessarily characteristic of British and European naturalistic works. Charles Child Walcutt, for example, in *American Literary Naturalism, A Divided Stream*, argues that American naturalism at the end of the nineteenth century displays a tension between, on one hand, idealism, progressivism, and social radicalism, and, on the other, mechanistic determinism (10). He further suggests that such contradictions exist in every piece of American naturalism: a tension between hope and despair, rebellion and apathy, defying nature and submitting to it, god as science and god as devil, and man's striving and admitting defeat (17). In summary, says Walcutt, "All 'naturalistic' novels exist in a tension between determinism and its antithesis" (29). In addition, Lilian Furst considers dualism to be intrinsic to naturalism, suggesting that naturalism is torn between "materialism and idealism, between pessimism and optimism" (quoted in Howard 37), and June Howard points out that naturalism contains elements of determinism as well as opposing elements of reformism, sensationalism, and assertions of human will (40).

Furthermore, Donald Pizer, in *Realism and Naturalism in Nineteenth-Century American Literature*, appears to agree with Walcutt when he claims that a keynote of the fiction of this period is a tension between actuality and hope, between man's limitations—imposed by his biological past and sociological present—and his stature as a creature of significance and worth. In addition, Pizer characterizes the subject matter of naturalism as an intermingling of contradictory elements: the commonplace and the sensational, the humanly ennobling and the humanly degrading (11–12). Referring specifically to Frank Norris, Pizer claims that these tensions and contradictions in naturalism are what Norris characterizes as "the romance of the commonplace" (12).

More recently, Lee Clark Mitchell, in *Determined Fictions: American Literary Naturalism*, reiterates the key concept of tension or contradiction in relation to characters in late-nineteenth-century naturalistic fiction. According to Mitchell, each text "defines a contradiction in its central character, between a self-image as an autonomous, integrated, freely willing agent, and the narrative's revelation of him as no more than a set of conflicting desires" (xv). In essence, naturalism is an assault on the reader's assumption of a moral self (xvi). Furthermore, claims Mitchell, naturalistic characters cannot refrain from action; they have a compulsion to act in predictable ways, which undermines their opportunities for choice (17). Repetition is therefore a key device in naturalistic fiction because it helps to show lack of self-control; involuntary repetition creates and reinforces a sense of helplessness (21).

Each of these critics identifies tension and/or contradiction as a central element in American naturalism, and Sasa's main argument regarding the femme fatale in naturalistic texts identifies a similar tension. According to Sasa, the femme fatale of naturalistic writers "is caught in the tension between the need to be free and the necessity of being determined." Each of the women Sasa examines is optimistic at the outset. Out of determination and hope, she strives to accomplish her essentially selfish goals in life, but she is ultimately defeated by her lack of true agency and circumstances or forces beyond her control. In essence, she evolves from victimizer to victim.

Either consciously or unconsciously, the femmes fatales of naturalistic fiction capture their male victims and alter their fates. Almost from the first day they meet, Frank Norris' McTeague is captivated by the charms of Trina. When Trina lies "unconscious and helpless and very pretty" and "absolutely without defense" (27) in his dental chair, McTeague is barely able to control himself. His sexual instincts are aroused to such an extent that he cannot resist kissing her "grossly, full on the mouth" (28). His behavior is beastly: "the sudden panther leap of the animal, lips drawn, fangs aflash, hideous, monstrous, not to be resisted" (28). Most critics portray Trina in this scene as the innocent victim of McTeague's animal nature, but after they are married, roles gradually reverse and Trina becomes the predator with McTeague as her prey. First, she persuades him to change his habits, then she makes financial decisions for him and refuses to share her lottery winnings with him, and finally she robs him of his pride and self-esteem. In essence, Trina emasculates McTeague. Therefore, although Trina does not appear to be a femme fatale at the outset, she clearly uses her wiles to manipulate McTeague into thinking and behaving as to how she wants him.

Ultimately, though, all of Trina's efforts are futile. As she becomes obsessed with hoarding money and refuses to sympathize with or help alleviate her husband's plight, McTeague grows increasingly alienated and the marriage becomes unbearable for him. Thus, Trina falls victim to her own greed and McTeague's eventual rebellion against her. First he takes her money, then her life.

Sasa convincingly traces a similar trajectory for female protagonists in other naturalistic texts. Like Trina, Theodore Dreiser's Carrie begins as optimistic and innocent. She arrives in Chicago seeking the American Dream. But Carrie learns quickly that the city is a man's world, and the key to her success is attaching herself to the right male. First, she charms Drouet and relies on him for financial support, but she soon recognizes his limitations and sets her sights on a better prospect, George Hurstwood. Not realizing that Hurstwood is married, Carrie captivates him to the extent that his behavior becomes irrational. Hurstwood "looked at his lovely prize, so beautiful, so winsome, so difficult to be won, and made strange resolutions. His passion had gotten to that stage now where it was no longer colored with reason" (163). He promises Carrie anything, even marriage, in order to seal his victory. Recklessly, he steals money from his employer and abandons his family in order to run off to New York City with his prize. Carrie's radiance has dazzled him and blinded him: "Hurstwood could not keep his eyes from Carrie. She seemed the one ray of sunshine in all his troubles. Oh, if she would only love him wholly…how happy he would be!…He would not care" if he lost everything (228).

Ironically, Hurstwood does lose everything in New York, including Carrie. Once Carrie realizes her mistake, she abandons the floundering and pathetic Hurstwood and becomes self-reliant, recognizing that she can use her charms on a larger scale by channeling them into her roles in musical comedy. Although Carrie seems to rise in the novel, Dreiser shows her to be a victim of her own dissatisfaction at the end. Forever rocking and dreaming, Carrie is destined to search continually for the vague happiness that always seems just beyond her reach. Although she has gained money and fame, like Fitzgerald's Jay Gatsby, she can never attain the elusive goal that is symbolized by the green light on the other side of the bay.

Ultimate dissatisfaction is also the fate of Nella Larsen's Helga Crane, another of Sasa's femmes fatales. Helga almost seems bipolar as her moods swing from optimistic and deliriously happy to dissatisfied and desperate for change. Although Helga frequently captivates men, most notably Swedish artist Axel Olsen and American academic Robert Anderson, she either loses interest in them or rationalizes rejecting their proposals. Transformed by her Swedish aunt and uncle into an exotic creature with gaudy plumage, Helga, a mulatta, is irresistible to her portrait painter Olsen. Olsen reveals his uncontrolled passion for Helga as he proposes marriage to Helga: "It may be that with you, Helga, for wife I will become great. Immortal. Who knows? I didn't want to love you, but I had to" (86–87). Even Olsen's portrait of Helga suggests that his view of her is colored by his passion for her. Helga believes that the portrait does not resemble her at all: "It wasn't, she contended, herself at all, but some disgusting sensual creature with her features" (89). Even her maid confirms Helga's view of the portrait, exclaiming, "I don't like that picture. It looks bad, wicked" (89). Clearly, Olsen has fallen victim to the femme fatale, for this is the image of Helga displayed in the portrait.

When Helga returns to New York City for her best friend Anne's wedding, she captivates another victim, this time her friend's new husband, Robert Anderson. Despite his recent marriage, Anderson has been fascinated by Helga ever since she was a teacher at Naxos where he was principal. Bumping into Helga in the hallway at a cocktail party, Anderson can no longer resist Helga's spell: "He stooped and kissed her, a long kiss, holding her close" (104). Although Helga, at first, responds to the kiss with reciprocal passion, she quickly recognizes her error and pushes Anderson away. Anderson too regrets his impulsive behavior and, a few days later, apologizes for his indiscretion. Nevertheless, Helga's power over him is evident.

Despite Helga's considerable power as femme fatale, she is never able to achieve personal happiness that lasts more than a couple of years. Becoming dissatisfied and restless, she is constantly impelled to move on—to a new state, a new city, a new country, a new relationship—and she eventually succumbs to her own fruitless searching and lack of self-knowledge. Although she is optimistic about her future as she enters each new situation, even her marriage to a southern minister, Helga realizes at the end of the novel that her marriage to Reverend Pleasant

Green and her roles as housewife and mother have trapped her in a fate from which there will be no escape. Caught in metaphorical quicksand and sinking fast, the femme fatale has been reduced to a victim of both church and patriarchy.

Therefore, *The Femme Fatale in American Literature* identifies power and agency in several female characters that have previously been labeled as weak. By showing these women in a new light, Sasa emphasizes that they are not primarily victims but strong women who have the potential to grow even stronger. Aware of the power of their sexuality, they use their feminine wiles to both captivate and manipulate their male victims. They also serve as forerunners of the New Woman that will populate the novels of the next generation of American writers. Unlike the "New Woman," however, the femme fatale of naturalism is eventually destined for either disillusionment or failure because the writer's deterministic vision seals her fate.

Professor Ronald Emerick
Department of English
Indiana University of Pennsylvania

WORKS CITED

Dreiser, Theodore. *Sister Carrie.* 1900. New York: Bantam, 1982.

Howard, June. *Form and History in American Literary Natural-ism.* Chapel Hill: University of North Carolina Press, 1985.

Larsen, Nella. *Quicksand and Passing.* Ed. Deborah E. McDowell. New Brunswick, NJ: Rutgers University Press, 1986.

Mitchell, Lee Clark. *Determined Fictions: American Literary Naturalism.* New York: Columbia University Press, 1989.

Norris, Frank. *McTeague.* 1899. New York: New American Library, 1964.

Pizer, Donald. *Realism and Naturalism in Nineteenth-Century American Literature.* Rev. ed. Carbondale: Southern Illinois University Press, 1984.

Walcutt, Charles Child. *American Literary Naturalism, A Divided Stream.* Minneapolis: University of Minnesota Press, 1956.

ACKNOWLEDGMENTS

I am greatly indebted to a number of special individuals who have guided me and helped me write and publish this book. My source of inspiration is my dear and loving husband, friend, and companion Muhammad, to whom I owe my eternal gratitude. Muhammad has stood by me and has always believed in me. I thank my three dear children, Noor, Yousef, and Sara for their unconditional love and their joyful laughter.

I wish to thank Dr. Ron Emerick for his insight, guidance, and support during my study at Indiana University of Pennsylvania. I also wish to thank Dr. Karen Dandurand and Dr. Malcolm Hayward for their insightful remarks and advice.

The completion of this book was dependent upon the support of a network of family members and close friends. Special thanks to my father, mother, brother, and sister for their prayers and encouragement. I mention a few dear friends who have a special place in my heart: Nidaa Abu Saymeh, Nadia Abu-Saymeh, Abeer Khanfar, Jehan Zitawi, and Lisa Matson are all true friends who have never failed me. I have always looked up to and aspired to be like my two special English instructors: Mrs. Susan Jarrah and Dr. Fadia Suyoufie.

To Muhammad, Noor, Yousef, and Sara: I love you.

To my father and my mother: May God bless and keep you in good health.

To my brother Issa and my sister Ghadeer: You are the best.

To my dear friends: Thank you for your friendship and for believing in me.

To my distinguished teachers and professors who have provided me with a wealth of information and who have, above all, taught me to have faith in myself: Thank you.

Last but not least, I wish to thank Cambria Press for providing me with the opportunity to publish this work. My special thanks go to Ms. Toni Tan for her guidance and help throughout the entire process.

THE FEMME FATALE
IN AMERICAN LITERATURE

CHAPTER 1

THE FEMME FATALE
IN AMERICAN NATURALISM:
AN INTRODUCTION

American naturalism has not only created a new type of man to be carefully read, studied, and understood, but it has also created a new type of woman. This book focuses on the representation of women in American naturalism and argues that women in American naturalism are often represented as femmes fatales. Although the femme fatale is not new to literary texts, she is fabricated and reconstructed according to the needs of this literary movement. This book focuses on the representation of the femmes fatales in three texts written during the height of the naturalistic movement: Frank Norris' *McTeague*, Theodore Dreiser's *Sister Carrie*, and Kate Chopin's *The Awakening*.

The traditional matter, themes, and forms of earlier American naturalistic fiction continued into the twentieth century and are visible in works such as Upton Sinclair's *The Jungle*, Theodore Dreiser's *An American Tragedy*, Ernest Hemingway's *The Sun Also Rises*, John Steinbeck's *The Grapes of Wrath*, Richard Wright's *Black Boy*, and Hemingway's *The Old Man and the Sea*. This book will include Nella Larsen's *Quicksand* as an example of a literary text written in the twentieth century that still carries the seeds and the themes inherent in the naturalistic movement.

Through examining the depiction of the femme fatale's heredity and environment, the book examines how biological determinism is affecting these women's characters and how it is leading them to the femme fatale path. This analysis assists in determining why, how, and at what point each woman decides to become a femme fatale. By examining works written by both male and female authors in the late nineteenth century and early twentieth century, this book demonstrates that this literary movement has both created and needed the femme fatale.

The threatening acts and aggressive attitudes of the women examined in this study are associated with their heredity and environment. Each of the women discussed is struggling in one way or another and is trying desperately to fight back against the suffocating constraints of heredity and environment. In order for these women to fight back, they are choosing to use their sexual appeal. This analysis focuses on the emergence of the femme fatale in American naturalism by analyzing the background, heredity, environment, and experiences of the female character.

The book analyzes how each of these femmes fatales is formed through her refusal to allow the environment and heredity to take control of her life. The question of whether or not these femmes fatales have succeeded in overcoming heredity and environment is a primary focus in this book. I argue that, even though these women struggle and may at some point succeed in overcoming these two pivotal forces, they, nevertheless, can never rid themselves of the strong grip of these forces. They choose to become femmes fatales in an attempt to liberate themselves from their backgrounds and the cruel surrounding environment in which they are captured. However, they end up not only entrapping and destroying the men around them, but also devastated and crushed themselves.

This study examines the female characters' individual backgrounds, their ambitions and aspirations, and their states of mind that lead them to decide to use their sexuality in order to fulfill their ambitions. It also examines how these women become dangerous and even deadly both to the men they encounter and to themselves. Through analyzing the writers' roles in creating this type of women, this book examines the affiliation between the psychological, sociological, and cultural formations within the time frame when the texts were written. These factors are important in the understanding of why the writers needed to create this new type of dangerous, alluring women. I assert that the depiction of women within American naturalism as femmes fatales functions as a part of the writers' ideological constructions. As the state of mind of each of these women is examined, the dominant cultural ideologies will also be investigated. I argue that the writers discussed in this book present women as femmes fatales as a way of showing why and how these women want to break free from biological determinism and the surrounding environment in which they find themselves entrapped. The depiction of aggressive and even deadly behavior in these women conveys the writers' critiques of biological determinism and social construction through the narratives. My examination focuses on the rationale for the female protagonists' hopes to move outside the prison of biological determinism and the surrounding environment.

In my analysis of the femme fatale in American naturalism, I also examine the role the writer plays in the formation of this figure. In the representation of the femme fatale figure in American naturalism, it is typical that both the male and female writers portray individuals living within imprisoned walls of heredity and environment. Moreover, both male and female writers show individuals struggling to break free. Yet, despite the common ground shared by the authors I have chosen for this work, there are differences between the writings of the male authors and the writings of the female authors.

The male authors represent the femme fatale characters as victims who gradually turn into victimizers, but they represent the male characters primarily as the victim of the femme fatale. Throughout the chapters, I point out how the femme fatale is formed, but I also focus on the effects the femme fatale is producing on herself and on others. Frank Norris and Theodore Dreiser, for example, lay emphasis on the imprisonment of McTeague and Hurstwood not only in the tangled web of heredity and environment, but also in the tangled web that the femme fatale creates for these men. Thus, the male writers show men doubly imprisoned, and the amalgamation of heredity, environment, and the spell the femme fatale creates brings about the male charcters' degeneration and ultimate destruction.

Reversibly, women authors approach the femme fatale issue from a different perspective. Yes, women are constricted because of the effects of heredity and environment. But they also have to deal with the constraints of living within a patriarchal culture and society. This is especially evident in Kate Chopin's *The Awakening*. As a result of her imprisonment within the patriarchal domain, Edna seeks an escape. And for her to escape, she deliberately chooses to use her beauty and charm. In Nella Larsen's *Quicksand*, Helga Crane is cursed because of the limitations imposed upon her by heredity, environment, society, and the color of her skin. Therefore, she chooses the same path that other femmes fatales have chosen. Like in Edna's case, we are made more aware of Helga's suffering than we are of the male characters' suffering in the novel.

Therefore, this study, in its examination of each of the femme fatale figures discussed, shows how male authors such as Frank Norris and Theodore Dreiser, writing within the tradition of American naturalism, mention but undermine the economic, political, social, and psychological oppression of women in order to foreground the suffering of the male character. On the other hand, writers like Kate Chopin and Nella Larsen reinforce the economic, political, social, and psychological oppression of their women characters and subtly attempt at justifying the course of action that these women choose as victims of the combined forces of sexism, heredity, and environment. Elaine Showalter explains in her article "Feminist Criticism in the Wilderness," "[W]omen's writing is a 'double-voiced discourse' that always embodies the social, literary, and cultural heritages of both the muted and the dominant…" (263).

BACKGROUND AND DEFINITIONS OF THE FEMME FATALE

In literature, the femme fatale has existed for centuries, and her image has developed according to the demands and needs of each literary movement. Examples of literary femmes fatales range in time from Chaucer's Wife of Bath in *The Canterbury Tales* created in the fifteenth century, to Hawthorne's Beatrice in "Rappacinni's Daughter," and into the twentieth century to include figures such as Lady Brett Ashley in *The Sun Also Rises*. Basically, the femme fatale is an archetype of an alluring, dangerous woman, determined to control and destroy. A typical femme fatale figure is best exemplified in John Keats' ballad "La Belle Dame Sans Merci:"

> I met a lady in the meads,
> Full beautiful, a fairy's child;
> Her hair was long, her foot was light,
> And her eyes were wild.
> …
> And there she lulled me asleep,
> And there I dream'd—Ah! Woe betide!
> The latest dream I ever dream'd
> On the cold hill's side.
> …
> I saw pale kings, and princes too,
> Pale warriors, death pale were they all;
> They cried—"La belle dame sans merci
> Hath thee in thrall!"

Keats' ballad tells the story of a knight destroyed by his love for the typical, archetypal femme fatale. The "knight at arms" has strayed in a world that has been toppled. He explains why he is alone and loitering. Having been lulled asleep by the enchantress, the knight has a dreadful vision in which a kingdom is held captive by an evil temptress. The poem is replete with anxiety as the woman destroys kings, princes, and warriors. She reduces the most powerful members of society to powerless, insignificant men, whereas she herself remains intact, powerful, and unaffected by her own doing.

But who exactly is the femme fatale? The femme fatale is typically classified as a siren, an irresistibly attractive woman, especially one who leads men into dangerous or disastrous situations. *The Grolier International Dictionary* defines the femme fatale as "a woman whose seductive charms may lead a man into compromising or dangerous situations" (483). The femme fatale in American naturalism is like any typical femme fatale—a seductive woman who displays power over a male character and who brings about change and destruction to the male characters she encounters. However, the femme fatale in American naturalism is not deadly. Only one of the male victims discussed in this study ends up dead, namely, Hurstwood in *Sister Carrie*. None of the femmes fatales discussed in this book is a murderess. However, all of these dangerous women are (in)directly responsible for the downfall of their male counterparts. But what distinguishes the femme fatale in American naturalism is that she ends up destroying herself. All of the femmes fatales discussed in this study are partially responsible for their downfalls and ultimate defeat.

Although the archetype of the femme fatale does not have an accurate definition, some common features of the femme fatale can be established. First of all, this woman embodies an unusual and fascinating beauty which sets her apart from other women and allows her to easily attract men. Because of this, the femme fatale employs her beauty to influence and entrap male characters. She often has a majestic, provocative aura about her, and her physical appearance is uniquely captivating. She generally has pale or white skin with a translucent quality which symbolizes an inexplicable, ethereal presence. The color of her hair and eyes is typically dark, contrasting with the skin's paleness. Her eyes are captivating to the male; also, her hands fascinate the male character, who notices their positions and movements. The colors red and black are symbolically used to represent the type's power. Because of her typical movement outside the boundaries of convention, she creates controversy in society; usually some characters in the literary work oppose the course of action that she undertakes. In addition, this woman seldom can or wants to perform the tasks of a nurturing and caring mother. Finally, although the femme fatale does not have to murder or destroy the male character, she does bring about a psychological change or an ominous change in him or in the quality of his life. Patrick Bade outlines the characteristics of the femmes fatales and asserts that femmes fatales are "pale, proud, mysterious, idol-like, full of perverse desires yet cold at heart" (8). These attributes summarize the common characteristics of this literary type. A combination of these characteristics suggests the presence of a femme fatale. In this book, I look for and examine these characteristics in each of the female protagonists being discussed.

Background and Definitions of American Naturalism
In American naturalism, characters are seen as helpless products of heredity and environment. Realism and naturalism have often been seen as two interrelated literary movements which objectively depict man's position as well as man's limitations.

In *The Beginnings of Naturalism in American Fiction*, Lars Ahnebrink provides definitions of both realism and naturalism. He defines realism as "a manner and method of composition by which the author describes normal, average life in an accurate and truthful way," whereas naturalism "is a manner and method of composition by which the author portrays life as it is in accordance with the philosophic theory of determinism" (vi). Ahnebrink outlines the differences between the realist and the naturalist: "In contrast to a realist, a naturalist believes that man is fundamentally an animal without free will. To a naturalist, man can be explained in terms of the forces, usually heredity and environment, which operate upon him" (vii).

Furthermore, Ahnebrink provides a useful historical and social context of American naturalism. Ahnebrink analyzes the social, philosophical, and literary backgrounds of this movement: "Gradually, American literature began to reflect the changes wrought in America by the rise of industrialism, the advance of science, the westward march of settlement, and the closing of the frontier" (14).

Ahnebrink's examination of historical and cultural information about naturalism has been useful in examining the cultural context and other background information. These cultural, social, and historical contexts are relevant to the formation of the femme fatale in this literary movement. Moreover, Ahnebrink's statement of the problem of free will is central to the study of the femme fatale:

> According to...naturalists, man has no free will; either external or internal forces, environment, or heredity control him and determine his behavior, for which he is not responsible. This belief is called determinism and is fundamental in naturalism. There are, of course, different stages of determinism, because a writer may not be a confirmed determinist, but a determinist only to a certain degree. All determinists believe, of course, in the existence of the will, but the will is often enslaved on account of various reasons. (184–185)

Although Ahnebrink here is focusing primarily on the naturalistic writer, the same can be said of the naturalistic character. The femme fatale is a determined character living in a determined world, yet whether or not she does have a will of her own and to what extent her will overcomes her determinism are two of the main focuses of this book.

Donald Pizer, in "Late Nineteenth-Century American Naturalism," proposes "a modified definition of late-nineteenth-century

American Naturalism" and believes that the naturalistic novel should not be read as superficial or reductive. The naturalistic novel

> suggests that even the least significant human being can feel and strive powerfully and can suffer the extraordinary consequences of his emotions...Naturalism reflects an affirmative ethical conception of life, for it asserts the value of all life by endowing the lowest character with emotion and defeat and with moral ambiguity, no matter how poor or ignoble he may seem. The naturalistic novel derives much of its aesthetic effect from these contrasts. (*American* 83)

The contrasts outlined by Pizer are essentially the contrasts that I address. The femme fatale in American naturalism is an emotional, sensitive character who begins as an innocent victim in the naturalistic world. Once heredity and environment seek to control this innocent victim, she becomes the victimizer who strives to overcome. One of her methods of fighting back is by victimizing men. She is eventually defeated by stronger forces; yet, at the same time, the fact that she has attempted to fight back may be seen as a victory in itself. All of these processes occur within a tangled web of "moral ambiguities."

In *The Light of Common Day: Realism in American Fiction*, Edwin H. Cady argues that man in realistic writings eventually reaches a moral vision, and thus, the literature of realism becomes "a literature of moral illumination" (36). On the other hand, Cady believes that man in naturalistic writings is a brute, exposed to socioeconomic factors that are more powerful and destructive than he is: "Man was reduced to the merest organism fighting meaninglessly, at the mercy of chance and force, to foredoomed loss" (47). I argue that socioeconomic factors surrounding these women are essential in creating the femme fatale.

In addition, Lee Clark Mitchell, in *Determined Fictions: American Literary Naturalism*, argues that protagonists in realistic writings assume a sense of responsibility; the naturalistic characters, on the other hand, lack the sense of will and responsibility associated with realistic characters, hence their impulsiveness and irresponsible actions (3).

Furthermore, John J. Conder, in *Naturalism in American Fiction: The Classic Phase*, examines American literary naturalism as a movement and traces the idea of "the free-will determinist" in this literary movement (16). In his introductory chapter, Conder outlines the various interpretations of naturalism and asserts, "[T]here does exist an important body of fiction, once called naturalistic, that does indeed possess philosophic coherence, and that such coherence depends on the evolution of a concept of questioning man's freedom" (4). However, Conder suggests that this movement does not only question man's freedom,

> it can lead to more. The person who feels the compelling power of causal factors in human as well as nonhuman affairs might very well hone his vision to see man as both determined and free, irreconcilable though the oppositions between determinism and freedom of the will may seem. (10)

By examining certain naturalistic texts, Conder's strategies for interpreting the actions of these characters have helped me in validating my own theories with regard to the femme fatale. Is she a determined character, or is she a free agent with a will of her own? This book attempts to provide an answer as to whether or not the femmes fatales discussed in this study give way more to the free will or submit to the deterministic constraints present in their worlds.

Because realism is often seen as a precursor to naturalism, I begin by examining a number of wives in realistic texts. The wives that I examine in American realistic texts are Mrs. Lapham in William Dean Howells' *The Rise of Silas Lapham*, Mrs. Adams in Booth Tarkington's *Alice Adams*, and Mrs. Bart in Edith Wharton's *The House of Mirth*. These wives play a pivotal role in the destruction of their husbands and that wives such as these are paving the way for and giving birth to the stronger, more dangerous and threatening women in naturalistic writing the same way in which American realism has given birth to American naturalism.

In *The Rise of Silas Lapham*, the dominating effect Mrs. Lapham has on her husband becomes immediately visible as the interviewer is talking with Mr. Lapham in his office: "If my wife wasn't good enough to keep both of us straight, I don't know what would become of me" (7). This is the first time the reader is introduced to Mrs. Lapham, and as Mr. Lapham continues his life story to Bartley, he mentions the control his wife, Persis, has had over his life. Most important, Mrs. Lapham was his school teacher, a factor which is indicative of the controlling relationship she would later have on her husband. Being above him in education gives her more control over Mr. Lapham, and Mrs. Lapham never ceases to forget this factor in their marriage by constantly reminding him of his unworthiness and foolishness whenever she has the chance to do so.

Because of having the upper hand in this marriage, the wife manipulates her husband under the pretense of giving advice. For example, she urges him to take on a business partner in the paint business. We hear Silas explaining to Bartley, "My wife was at me all the time to take a partner—somebody with capital; but I couldn't bear the idea" (14). Yet, the reader senses her greed in the acquisition of wealth that this paint may incur for them: "Well, you hain't got a paint-mine, Silas Lapham; you've got a gold-mine" (9).

When Mr. Lapham follows her advice and takes on a partner, Mr. Lapham struggles with Mr. Rogers throughout the novel. Mrs. Lapham manipulates her husband in feeling sympathetic toward Mr. Rogers because Mr. Lapham had bought him out of their mutual business. She constantly reminds Silas of the wrong he has committed toward Mr. Rogers, making him feel guilty and allowing Mr. Rogers to come back into their lives. Yet, her purpose in doing so is to prove that she is right and he is wrong. The fact that she constantly strives to prove herself right takes us back to the idea that she was his school teacher, higher than he, more knowledgeable, and more experienced than he. By reasoning with Mr. Lapham time and time again about the unjustifiable wrongs he has committed against Mr. Rogers, Mrs. Lapham is in fact trying to prove that she is a better judge of character than her husband. When Silas finally gives in to the idea of making amends with Mr. Rogers by helping him out financially, she is satisfied only because Silas has given in to her opinion. "The lord has been good to you, Silas...I believe he's interfered this time; and I tell you, Silas, it ain't always he gives people a chance to make it up to others in this life" (107). The ruin of Silas begins because he follows his wife's advice in the beginning and takes on a partner and ends because he follows her advice and makes amends with Mr. Rogers.

Toward the end of the novel when Mr. Lapham is crumbling and is in desperate need of guidance and support, he finally chooses not to confide in and trust his wife. This, I believe, is part of the growth of Mr. Lapham. He finally comes to the realization that he has been misled by his wife, first by making amends with Mr. Rogers, and second in building the house on Beacon Street. The novel concludes with Mr. Lapham's moral victory, and it also concludes with the realization that his wife has been a part of his moral decline. Only when he avoids her at the end of the novel is he able to make the right, moral decisions of not selling his worthless milling property to the English buyers and of not selling his paint works to a New York agent who is unaware of the declining market for Lapham's mineral paint. The narrator informs us, "Lapham stole a troubled glance at his wife and saw that there was no hope in her" (269). When she tries to offer him advice about the two issues, he refuses to let her dominate him any more, telling her, "[She] couldn't do any good" (271). This is the point when Mrs. Lapham's student is finally able to make his own decisions without the interference of his teacher, Mrs. Lapham, hence the growth of Silas Lapham. He breaks free from his teacher.

The novel ends where it begins. In the beginning of the novel, we hear Mr. Lapham telling Bartley about their farm and the simple life they had previously enjoyed before the paint had been discovered and before the greed and manipulation of Mrs. Lapham grew. In the end, Mr. Lapham is back on the farm, leading a very simple life. In between the events, Mrs. Lapham plays a significant role in the financial catastrophes that happen to her husband. The reader does see Mrs. Lapham as a good person in many instances throughout the novel, yet she is partially responsible for the cascading series of financial disasters brought upon their family. Her misjudgment, hesitancy, greed, and lack of faith in her husband lead him to disastrous financial situations. He is able to recover once he finally refuses to allow her to interfere with his decisions. Therefore, he achieves a moral victory, and the ending of the novel is a happy one.

Another wife who plays a significant role in the downfall of her husband is Mrs. Adams in Booth Tarkington's *Alice Adams*. Although the novel revolves around Alice's hopes and tactics in attracting a wealthy husband, it also presents the dilemmas and struggles Alice has to put up with because of her devious mother, Mrs. Adams. Alice is not the only victim of her mother, but it is Mr. Adams who is mainly victimized by his wife.

The novel depicts the disintegration of a lower-middle-class family. Mr. Adams works for the company of the wealthy Mr. Lamb and has to take some time off from work because he falls sick. During his time of convalescence, Mrs. Adams taunts her husband and urges him "to find something really good to get into" (10), very determined that "he mustn't go back to that old hole again" (11). Like Mrs. Lapham, Mrs. Adams uses her children as an excuse to motivate him to better their lives and their social standing. She struggles throughout the novel to convince him to build a glue factory and, consequently, leave his employer, who was originally the one who had come up with the idea of building a glue factory and, 20 years ago, had asked Mr. Adams to help him in implementing his plans. When Mr. Adams finally gives in to his wife's ideas, he is devastated by his employer, Mr. Lamb, who builds an adjacent, bigger, and more advanced glue factory. Eventually, Mr. Lamb makes peace with Mr. Adams and buys him out of the business, and Mr. Adams returns to his previous employment with the Lamb Company.

As a result of the never-ending nagging of Mrs. Adams, Alice is confused and faces serious questions as to where she stands. When she meets Arthur Russell, she pretends to be the daughter of a wealthy businessman and carries on her role as such until he discovers that she has been lying to him all along. She loses Arthur as a potential husband but grows morally at the end when she finally learns to understand and accept the position of her father.

The mother, on the other hand, never does learn to accept her husband's employment and financial situation. Although she realizes that her husband has been ultimately defeated by the richer and the more powerful, she constantly seeks to shape him in accordance with her own beliefs. The idea of framing is reiterated in the novel as a means of showing what Mrs. Adams really strives for. In more than one situation, she tells her daughter, "If we don't get him [Mr. Adams] into the right frame of mind now, we never will" (17). As an example of a disruptive wife, Mrs. Adams hopes to formulate, shape, and reconstruct Mr. Adams' frame of mind according to her own beliefs and aspirations. Her ideas of framing his mind are in contrast to Alice's ideas on what her mother is doing to him. To Alice, this is "ding-donging at him" and "hammering at him" (18–20). The daughter is able to see that her mother is trying to use the father, unfairly, for her purpose of having more money, as it is the mother's belief that "money is family" and that "money is at the bottom of it all" (210–212).

Like *The Rise of Silas Lapham*, the novel ends where it begins. Mr. Adams is in bed sick, and Mrs. Adams is bewailing her fortunes and her husband. She does not, however, learn from the mistakes she has committed against herself and her husband. She does not undergo a process of moral growth, and she does not realize that her complaints will no longer be heard.

Mrs. Bart in Edith Wharton's *The House of Mirth* provides another example of a manipulative wife, yet she is different from both Mrs. Lapham and Mrs. Adams in that she is also a manipulative mother. Although Mrs. Bart's actions are limited in the novel, they are very significant in the destruction of her husband and of her daughter as well.

By insisting on not being expected to "live like a pig" (31), Mrs. Bart leads her husband to his death. Although she is a member of a middle-class family, she is always persistent in not appearing as one. Her need for having dinner banquets, traveling to Europe, wearing expensive clothes, and having flowers on the dinner table each night means more to Mrs. Bart than the well-being of her husband. Driven by wanting more and more money to come into her life, the mother instills in her daughter the values of the materialistic world and teaches her never to be satisfied without money and without the luxuries that come along with money. On the day of his ruin, Mr. Bart walks in on his wife and daughter while the two of them are discussing the importance of having enough lilies on the dinner table. Lily, who "hate[s] to see faded flowers at luncheon," and Mrs. Bart, who "had no tolerance for scenes which were not of her own making," do not realize the fact that Mr. Bart is "ruined" (33). Not only do they not realize this, but they also do not want to sympathize with the husband's bankruptcy and financial ruin: "To his wife, he no longer counted: he had become extinct when he ceased to fulfill his purpose" (34). The fact that Mrs. Bart has been mainly concerned with her husband because of the income he brings into the family shows how deeply ungrateful his wife is. Little do we know about her husband's subsequent death, but we learn that the wife still has one solace amid her poverty, and it is the contemplation of her daughter's beauty: "She studied it with a kind of passion, as though it were some weapon she has slowly fashioned for her vengeance. It was the last asset in their fortune, the nucleus around which their life was to be rebuilt" (35). She "used to say to her [daughter] with a kind of fierce vindictiveness, 'But you'll get it all back—you'll get it all back with your face.'" (30).

The novel centers around Lily's destruction and ends with Lily's defeat. Lily drifts alone in the world, yet is always dependent on the values her mother has passed on to her: "I am horribly poor—and very expensive. I must have a great deal of money" (29). Her destruction is gradual as she moves downward from one social class to another. She mingles with the aristocrats and the rich and powerful leaders of high society. When she tries to keep up with these wealthy acquaintances by drifting from one party to another, she accumulates gambling and dressmaking debts. When her aunt Julia Peniston learns of her debts, she disowns her. As a result, Lily is forced to earn her living first as a secretary and then as a seamstress, only to fail in both jobs because she lacks adequate training and physical endurance. She is unable to survive economically by her independent efforts as a wage earner. Like her father's death, Lily's suicide at the end of the novel is a result of her mother's influence.

Mrs. Lapham, Mrs. Adams, and Mrs. Bart are three examples of controlling, demanding wives who play a significant role in the destruction of their husbands. Given the fact that all three wives are mainly concerned with the money that can be generated from their husbands' labor, all three wives are what I label as "deadly wives." They care more about the financial aspect of their marriages than they do about the well being of their husbands and children. The destructive wives in American realism discussed in this introduction serve as a preliminary version of more dangerous and deadly women that appears in American naturalism.

The Femme Fatale and American Naturalism
This book takes a closer look at some of the women produced in American naturalistic writings. These women are facing a dilemma as to their place in the universe. They are enslaved to their determinism, and yet at the same time, they are searching for their freedom and individuality. They want to rebel against their surrounding environment, to break free from dominance, and to have a will of their own. Paradoxically, they are controlled by their surrounding environment, they are dominated in every possible way, and they do not have a will of their own.

These irreconcilable oppositions are what give birth to the femme fatale—the kind of woman who, by using her sexuality, is simultaneously determined, yet free. She lacks freedom of the will, yet, at the same time, she controls freedom of the will. She is a victim, yet she is also a victimizer. She is a slave to circumstances, yet she aspires to be free. She is an innocent, harmless, dominated individual in society, yet she is devilish and domineering. All of these contradictions found in this femme fatale are the product of this literary movement. It has created this type of woman—the femme fatale who is caught in the tension between the need to be free and the necessity of being determined. In this way, the femme fatale in American naturalism may well be read in the context of Elaine Showalter's influential article "Feminist Criticism in the Wilderness." Showalter argues, "[T]he ways in which women conceptualize their bodies and their sexual and reproductive functions are intricately linked to their cultural environments" (259). The cultural environment is what compels the women in this study to decide to use the power of their femininity.

In my analysis of the femme fatale figure in American naturalism, I deliberately choose Trina Sieppe, Caroline Meeber, Edna Pontellier, and Helga Crane as representatives of this figure created because of this literary movement. I show, in my study, how these four women, despite their differences, share common ground. Therefore, throughout the chapters of this book, point by point comparisons between these women will be made. All the female protagonists have harsh battles to fight against heredity and environment. However, they refuse to become puppets of these dominating factors and emerge, as a result, as femmes fatales. Trina Sieppe is a victim of hereditary traits, Sister Carrie is a victim of the cruel materialistic city, Edna Pontellier is a victim of patriarchy, and Helga Crane is a victim of the color of her skin. All four victims decide to reverse their position from victim to victimizer. All four victims enjoy temporary victory. But, alas, all four victims do not enjoy perpetual victory.

Conder, who calls this type of character in American naturalism "the free-will determinist," poses an important question. Can free will and determinism co-exist? Which factor will eventually overcome the other, free will or determinism?

A close examination of the ending of each of the novels discussed assists in providing answers to such questions. In Frank Norris' *McTeague*, Trina Sieppe is brutally murdered by her husband. The murder signifies the defeat of Trina and asserts that biological determinism is stronger than free will. On the other hand, Edna Pontellier in Kate Chopin's *The Awakening* swims toward the open sea, allowing the environment to take full command of her life. Paradoxically, because she would not let heredity and environment control her, she decides to end her life. The ambiguous ending stems from the ambiguity from which the free will determinist is created. Caroline Meeber in Theodore Dreiser's *Sister Carrie* rocks herself in the rocking chair, thinking of how empty and fruitless her life is now after she has acquired wealth and fame. She ends up as a free agent in control of her life, yet she feels that her life has no meaning at this point without being determined and controlled. Finally, Helga Crane in Nella Larsen's *Quicksand* ends up entrapped in marriage and childbearing without the remotest possibility of ever getting back the freedom she enjoyed before being married. Ironically, she had believed that marriage would provide her with the freedom she had been looking for all along. Although each of the four novels ends differently, they all depict the female protagonists struggling in the ambiguity created by themselves for wanting to be free agents by being femmes fatales yet being controlled by their surrounding environment.

Therefore, this book brings together four different women created by four different male and female authors and subverts earlier criticism written about women in American naturalistic writings. Ahnebrink argues, "[T]he type of woman most frequently met with in naturalistic writing—such as…Trina—was generally weak, passive, often neurotic and hysterical, dominated by heredity and environment, ruled by passions and instincts, and lacking will power and brains." Ahnebrink contrasts the woman in naturalistic writings with the new, modern woman, who "possessed a will of her own and dominated men instead of being dominated by them" (220–221). I argue that the woman created in American naturalism is neither weak nor passive; neither is she, I believe, the New Woman who does have a will of her own. Rather, she is the strong, active, femme fatale who struggles to find a will of her own and who struggles to fight the heredity and environment by controlling and dominating the men she encounters.

A distinct line should be drawn between the femme fatale created by American naturalism, and the new, modern woman, both of whom were created at the end of the nineteenth century and the beginning of the twentieth century. Although the femme fatale as a literary type may seem to overlap in some ways with the New Woman of the turn of the century, they are, nevertheless, distinctly different.

According to Carroll Smith-Rosenburg, the "New Woman" was originally a term created by Henry James, who used it to describe characters such as Daisy Miller and Isabel Archer. These women are characterized as young, single, and refusing to submit themselves to social conventions. However, with characters such as Daisy Miller and Isabel Archer, these New Woman characters suffered the consequences of their autonomy. Smith-Rosenburg transposes James' literary phrase into a sociological and historical context but maintains James' focus on the New Woman's rejection of social conventions, her desire to be independent, and her roots in American society. She uses the phrase to refer to "a specific sociological and educational cohort of women who were born between the late 1850s and 1900," who "represented the new demographic trends of late marriages for bourgeois women," and who "reject[ed] conventional female roles and assert[ed] their right to a career, to a public vote, to visible power..." (176).

According to Smith-Rosenburg, the New Woman's most distinctive feature was education. Many young women saw in college education "an opportunity for intellectual self-fulfillment and for an autonomous role outside the patriarchal family" (247). Seeking an education would serve as a means of developing women's intelligence and, consequently, as a means of achieving success in the outside world. Thus, the woman would not be entrapped within the domestic sphere nor by her conventional role as wife and mother. Moreover, the New Woman sought employment opportunities once she had received an education—another step that would help her in achieving autonomy. Resenting restrictions that society imposed on women, the New Woman began to create alternative visions of female intellectual power, self-fulfillment, and nondomestic roles. By the early twentieth century, the New Woman had firmly established herself within the professional world that had traditionally been defined as a man's sphere (Smith-Rosenburg 176).

But who specifically is the New Woman? Smith-Rosenburg believes that women who were associated with the settlement-house movement, women educational reformers, and women writers and artists were the most visible of the New Women. However, she also believes that the phrase should also include many other less visible women teachers, social and medical workers, business women and so forth, as long as they lived economically and socially independent lives (177).

The femme fatale in American naturalism is not the New Woman's counterpart. The femme fatale's major adversary is the deterministic world in which she lives, and therefore, the femme fatale is the woman who necessarily has to rely on her sexuality in her attempt to liberate herself from the world in which she is entrapped. The main and most significant difference between the New Woman and the femme fatale of American naturalism is education. Women characters like Nan Prince in Sarah Orne Jewett's *A Country Doctor*, Dr. Zay in Elizabeth Stuart Phelp's *Dr. Zay*, and Iola Leroy in Frances E. W. Harper's *Iola Leroy* represent new, modern women who are seeking alternative views of matrimony and the domestic sphere by seeking education and careers that come as the result of education. Susan K. Harris comments on a number of these women protagonists, such as Nan Prince in *A Country Doctor*, asserting,

> [These women] prove to themselves—and most impor-
> tantly to the readers—that in fact they are capable of
> achievement beyond the home. For readers already pre-
> disposed toward women's movement out of the domestic
> sphere, they provide a strong incentive to explore alter-
> native possibilities. (200)

Harris concludes by asserting, "[B]y the mid-1870s, the passive self-abnegating female of early didactic novels had been transformed into an active, self-possessed, and politically conscious woman" (201).

Although both kinds of women were created at the turn of the twentieth century, and although they may seem to carry some similarities, the two types of women are not identical. All the women studied in this book seek economic independence. Trina wins the lottery by luck, yet she also has her own job of making Noah's ark animals. Carrie leaves her family behind and goes off to the big city to look for employment. Edna decides to paint and make a living out of that, and Helga is seen throughout the novel seeking employment. They all seek economic autonomy, yet they employ different means than the ones the New Woman has employed. The women studied here do not seek an education and therefore do not utilize their intellectual abilities. What they do utilize, though, is their sexuality. And for them to be economically independent having no academic background, they have to use and/or abuse the male characters they encounter along the way. Trina dates McTeague before she wins the lottery, and when she does win the lottery, she makes it clear to him that the money shall not be touched. Carrie lives with Drouet first and then Hurstwood in order to secure herself financially while being in the big industrial city. Once she gets a job, she abandons Hurstwood. Edna is securely married to Mr. Pontellier yet decides to leave him and make her own living by being an artist once she believes that she will be able to be with Robert Lebrun. Helga drifts here and there, searching for happiness, yet also searching for a means of being financially secure.

Both the New Woman and the femme fatale of American naturalism have battles to fight, but the battles they fight are extremely different from each other. Whereas the New Woman's main quest is to seek autonomy and independence from patriarchal authority, the femme fatale of American naturalism battles are not only against patriarchy, but also against heredity and environment. Due to the fact that the battles fought are different, the means of fighting are different as well. In fighting these battles, the New Woman utilizes her intellectual capabilities whereas the femme fatale utilizes her sexual appeal. The New Woman has no victims as she is battling for her individuality and autonomy. The femme fatale, on the other hand, victimizes the men she comes into contact with as she is battling against patriarchy, heredity, and environment.

In "Women as Superfluous Characters in American Realism and Naturalism," Jan Cohn argues that naturalistic novels relegate women to a very specific and very limited role in the novels:

> [C]haracterizations of women lose both individuality and vitality, and complexities of motivation are leveled to simplistic assumptions, while the female character is merely sketched and labeled in accord with popular stereotypes and with the narrative exigencies involved in depicting the conflicts facing the only real actor in this world—the money-making man. (156)

However, women in American naturalism are motivated and strong women who are fighting against the naturalistic world that they have found themselves entrapped in. All the women studied in this book are not merely agents in the world of the "money-making man," but they are employed and seek financial independence from the men around them. Moreover, as is the case with *McTeague* and *Sister Carrie*, it is the female characters that end up working and the male characters who are eventually unemployed and are begging for money from the "money-making" women.

Focusing mainly on canonical American literature, Judith Fryer, in *The Faces of Eve: Women in the Nineteenth Century American Novel*, argues that the American Eve cannot be contained in a single image, and therefore Fryer classifies women in American nineteenth-century literature into four different categories: Temptress, American Princess, Great Mother, and New Woman. Although Fryer's choice of literary texts is different from my choice, Fryer's theory of the temptress is similar to mine. She asserts, "[T]he dark lady, is for one thing, more than temptress: she has within her the seeds of liberation—her own and…vicariously her author's" (28). It is my opinion that in her attempt to liberate herself from heredity and environment, the femme fatale in American naturalism carries within her the "seeds of liberation" despite the fact that she does not come to a full liberation or a conquest of the stronger forces that control her life.

What is unique about this study is the fact that it shows the naturalistic woman in a new light and a new form. Although the naturalistic character in general has been seen as a puppet being controlled by the outer and stronger forces of heredity and environment, it is my intention to prove that naturalistic women do find a means of escape by using their sexuality and by choosing to become dangerous, destructive, and threatening women. At one point, these female protagonists seem to be able to subvert the stronger forces; yet at the end, the female characters' deaths, such as Edna's or Trina's, or their dead-in-life status, such as Carrie's and Helga's, can be seen as a defeat. This devaluation does not depict women's ability to transcend and to validate a better position for the naturalistic character. However, Trina's, Edna's, Carrie's, and Helga's aggressive actions and their quests show the reader the significance of the battles they are fighting, as well as their strategies to overcome heredity and environment.

Chapter 2 to chapter 5 examine the characteristics of the femme fatale in the female protagonists of the novels studied in this book. Each chapter also investigates the female protagonist's heredity and environment and tries to account for why these women choose to become deadly. In chapter 2, I look closely at the character of Trina in Norris' *McTeague*. A close reading of Trina's background and family shows how and why Trina decides to become a femme fatale. Trina plays a significant role in the degeneration of the already degenerated McTeague and is never satisfied until she eventually ruins herself and falls as his victim. Norris provides American naturalism with an example of a woman who, because of heredity and environment, is doomed to being fatal. As a result of being controlled, Trina seeks to take control of McTeague, first by bringing out his animalistic instincts, then by shaping him the way she wants him to be, and finally by controlling him financially with the money she has won and earned. As McTeague undergoes a process of degeneration, the femme fatale is in full command of the situation. Eventually, the femme fatale does lose control and ends up being murdered by her male victim.

Chapter 3 focuses on Caroline Meeber in Dreiser's *Sister Carrie*. By comparing and contrasting her to Trina, I show how she is similar to, yet, at the same time, different from Trina. She provides another example of a femme fatale who seeks to victimize men and make them fall in love with her because of her goal to seek control. Moreover, she is, in my opinion, responsible for the downfall of Hurstwood. Once Hurstwood encounters Carrie, his degeneration starts. The novel does not end with the death or murder of Carrie. Rather, it ends with Carrie being a dead-in-life character rocking herself in the rocking chair.

Chapter 4 discusses the character of Edna Pontellier in Chopin's *The Awakening*. Married with two children, this femme fatale is in need of more power in her life and therefore victimizes two male characters. I explore Edna's background and upbringing in this chapter. I also investigate why she decides to be a femme fatale, and finally, I examine her death/suicide.

Chapter 5 focuses on Helga Crane in Nella Larsen's *Quicksand*. Helga is different from the other female protagonists, as she is a mulatta, living in the twentieth century, who is suffering from loss of identity and cannot find a place for herself in the world. She chooses to become a femme fatale as a means of taking revenge on the world. Therefore, she seeks pleasure in making men fall in love with her. She has many male victims throughout the text, and like Carrie, ends up as a dead-in-life character.

Within these chapters, comparisons will be made among these four women to show that these women are similar in the battles they are facing, in their quests for liberation, and in their approach in fighting back. Despite the fact that I deal with each character's individual situation, the comparisons are made to show the reader these women characters should be looked at from a different perspective other than as mere victims, but rather as strong daring women who make an attempt at controlling their destiny by means of using their charm and beauty.

The concluding chapter in the book will provide other examples of dangerous women in American naturalistic writings. The conclusion of this study suggests that femmes fatales in American naturalism exist in various guises and are represented by both male and female naturalistic writers in order to show that the naturalistic women in particular do struggle to fight and escape the net that they are entrapped in. Although they do not succeed in most cases, the femmes fatales at least do try to overcome heredity and environment.

I hope that my analysis of the femme fatale in American naturalism is not read negatively. This book does not intend to highlight the femme fatale as having negative connotations. In examining the femme fatale, I seek possibilities for a construction of a broader view of the female characters in American naturalism. I assert that women in American naturalism are strong, daring, and determined women who refuse to merely be puppets of stronger forces. In order to do so, they rely on their sexuality and use, victimize, and abuse the men they encounter. However, in this whole process of fighting the external forces by using men, the femme fatale comes to the realization that heredity and environment are stronger than she has anticipated.

CHAPTER 2

TRINA "TOOK HER PLACE IN THE OPERATING CHAIR:" TRINA SIEPPE AS FEMME FATALE IN FRANK NORRIS' MCTEAGUE

Since the publication of *McTeague* in 1899, literary criticism has focused on McTeague's character, his brutality, his degeneration, and the naturalistic, deterministic world in which he lives. McTeague is regarded as a typical naturalistic character—a brute who relies heavily on his animalistic instincts, a character devoid of free will, a character who is eventually defeated because of his inability to free himself of the determining factors that operate upon him. Trina Sieppe has also been regarded by Lars Ahnebrink as an example of a determined character in a determined world—a character who is "weak, passive, often neurotic and hysterical, dominated by heredity and environment" (220). Yet Trina has never been regarded as a femme fatale with threatening behavior that plays an important role in McTeague's ultimate brutality and degeneration. She is constantly seen as the victim of her own hereditary traits and the victim of McTeague's inherited brutality as well, yet she is seldom seen as the catalyst that is responsible for bringing out all that is foul and evil in McTeague.

Frank Norris subtly and perhaps intentionally creates an example of a femme fatale in *McTeague*. The creation of this character serves two functions: First, the femme fatale is responsible for bringing out all that is evil in the male character and serves as a reminder that evil and foulness are part of the male's heredity. Second, by creating this type of woman, the naturalistic writer may be trying to suggest that naturalistic characters are finding a means of fighting back against their heredity and environment. I focus on three main areas in this chapter. I cite evidence from the text to prove that Trina is indeed a femme fatale. I examine Trina's heredity, environment, and background, as well as her threatening and menacing behavior. I also examine the effects this woman has on McTeague and argue that a great part of McTeague's degradation is caused by this femme fatale who is trying to shape and manipulate him according to her own desires and needs. I also argue that the depiction of the disastrous marriage of Trina and McTeague is intended on the part of the author to show the femme fatale in action and to show what she is capable of.

Trina, before her encounter with McTeague, lives in a controlling domestic realm. She is controlled by her parents, and she realizes that her parents are controlled by their inherited traits. She looks for a means of escape. She uses her charm on "the operating chair" and entraps McTeague (19). Instead of being controlled in a controlling environment, she decides to take full control of her husband, McTeague. She controls him sexually, psychologically, and financially. The femme fatale is in full command of the household. Her victim is McTeague. Ironically, she starts to lose control of the situation when the hereditary traits she has tried to escape from start to reappear when she wins the lottery. She begins to compulsively hoard, and in the process, loses control of McTeague. She brings about her own destruction and is murdered by the man she has chosen as her victim. This chapter traces the emergence of Trina as a femme fatale before the marriage, the complete construction of Trina as a femme fatale during the marriage, and the gradual and ulti-mate downfall of the femme fatale after Trina wins the lottery.

THE EMERGENCE OF THE FEMME FATALE

Norris introduces Trina in chapter 2 and provides a detailed description of her as Marcus Schouler, Trina's cousin, is intro-ducing her to McTeague. The femme fatale emerges from this description:

> Trina was very small and prettily made. Her face was round and rather pale; her eyes long and narrow and blue, like the half open eyes of a little baby; her lips and the lobes of her tiny ears were pale, a little suggestive of anemia; while across the bridge of her nose ran an ador-able little line of freckles. But it was to her hair that one's attention was most attracted. Heaps and heaps of blue-black coils and braids, a royal crown of swarthy bands, a veritable sable tiara, heavy, abundant, odorous. All the

> vitality that should have given color to her face seemed to have been absorbed by this marvelous hair. It was the coiffure of a queen that shadowed the pale temples of this little bourgeoise. So heavy was it that it tipped her head backward, and the position thrust her chin out a little. It was a charming poise, innocent, confiding, almost infantile.
>
> She was dressed all in black, very modest and plain. The effect of her pale face in all this contrasting black was almost monastic. (22)

Like the Medusa, who is charged with profound sensuality and physicality, the description of Trina juxtaposes her extraordinary beauty with her eminent threat. The passage demands close attention, for the description conjures the image of the typical femme fatale. First, Trina's hairstyle evokes an image of the sensuous woman. In creating this femme fatale, Norris' first step is making use of the fashion trends and the hairstyles that were prominent at the time. According to Mary Trasko in *Daring Do's*, in the 1880's, it became fashionable for women to grow their hair longer and longer until it reached their backs or even their knees. The women of the time were up to date on fashion trends and popular hairstyles from reading popular publications such as *Godey's Lady's Book*. The description of Trina's hair runs parallel to the prevailing hairstyle of the time: a small hat perched on the front of the head with the hair swept up in the back. The look of the time called for an abundance of hair which could be coiled and then spread up from the neck to the top of the head. Trasko asserts, "At the end of the [nineteenth] century, waves of free flowing hair, in romantic visions of evil, of the erotic, the decadent, and the femme fatale became the dominant themes of Art Nouveau..." (103).

Norris' second step in the making of this femme fatale is in describing her as a woman with an attractive figure, with big, expressive eyes, and a face of striking paleness contrasted with a mass of black hair. The pale skin and the association with the color black serve as a warning of the presence of the femme fatale. As a result of Trina's unusual beauty, men are easily attracted to Trina. We are made aware of Marcus Schouler's (her cousin) attraction to her charm and beauty: "He [Marcus], too, felt the charm of the little girl—the charm of the small, pale forehead; the little chin thrust out as if in confidence and innocence; the heavy odorous crown of black hair. He liked her immensely" (47).

McTeague, who has had no interest in women, becomes instantly attracted to her as well. Once McTeague is introduced to Trina, he is no longer occupied with his other bodily functions of eating, drinking, and sleeping. His world becomes toppled. He is fascinated and enchanted by Trina and, therefore, his sexuality is aroused. He has known other women before he has met the femme fatale, Trina, but none have had the effect that Trina has on McTeague: "These young girls disturbed and perplexed him. He did not like them, obstinately cherishing that intuitive suspicion of all things feminine—the perverse dislike of an overgrown boy" (22). The femme fatale mystifies and intrigues him:

> Little by little, by gradual, almost imperceptible degrees, the thought of Trina Sieppe occupied his mind from day to day, from hour to hour. He found himself thinking of her constantly; at every instant he saw her round, pale face; her narrow, milk-blue eyes; her little out-thrust chin; her heavy, huge tiara of black hair. At night he lay awake for hours under the thick blankets of the bed-lounge, staring upward into the darkness, tormented with the idea of her, exasperated at the delicate subtle mesh in which he found himself entangled. (25)

The femme fatale causes a physiological change in McTeague by bringing out his animalistic sexual desires. McTeague, whose only pleasures in life were "to eat, to smoke, to sleep, and to play upon his concertina" (6), now, and because of his encounter with the femme fatale, has something else to think about: "all at once he saw that there was something else in life besides concertinas and steam beer" (27).

The femme fatale also brings about a psychological change in McTeague by disrupting the order of his routinely monotonous life. In the beginning of the novel, Norris carefully documents McTeague's life as a dentist. McTeague's world is steadfastly organized around McTeague's occupation. Donald Pizer believes that McTeague's profession's "habitual tasks and minor successes represent the order and stability which McTeague requires, given his limited intelligence, if his life is to have any meaning and if it is not to disintegrate into the brutality which, in Norris' oft-repeated words, is in McTeague so close to the surface" (*The Novels of Frank* 76). As noted by Pizer, the fact that Norris is providing such details about the stable life of McTeague serves as an indicator that McTeague is perfectly content in his little dental parlor. However, if this order is disrupted, the brute in McTeague will undoubtedly emerge. The femme fatale disrupts this order, and she will ultimately pay the price for being responsible for bringing out the brute. In the first few encounters between McTeague and Trina, Norris more than once stresses the fact that Trina "took her place in the operating chair" (19, 22). It is beyond doubt that Trina is being operated on by McTeague, yet Trina herself is in the process of operating on McTeague. Taking her position "in the operating chair," she is in full control: "Suddenly the animal in the man stirred and woke; the evil instincts that were in him so close to the surface leaped to life, shouting and clamoring" (27).

In order to understand why Trina chooses to use her alluring charm to entrap McTeague, the reader must look closely at the environment which has created this femme fatale. The Sieppes, like the McTeagues, are a family preoccupied with their bodily functions. Of German-Swiss origin, the Sieppes are a family of six: the father, the mother, Trina, and three other children. In the first part of the novel, Norris not only makes the reader aware of the presence of the femme fatale, but he also stresses her background. The only thing the family does is eat. They eat greedily and hungrily, on picnics, at home, and during the wedding feast. The feast at the wedding best portrays their vulgarity and grotesqueness. Plates of food are brought in and quickly devoured. Eating and drinking are performed for the sake of eating and drinking. There was no enjoyment or celebration in the whole process. The air was thick and heavy with perspiration: "For two hours the guests ate, their faces red, their elbows wide, the perspiration beading their foreheads. All around the table, one saw the same incessant movement of jaws and the same uninterrupted sound of chewing" (133). They are animalistic human beings whose main concern is feeding their stomachs and, consequently, going to the bathroom.

Another grotesque image Norris provides about the Sieppes is the time when McTeague invites Trina and her family to the theater. Owgooste, Trina's younger brother, begins to feel uneasy because of his need to go to the bathroom. The mother ignores his urges until he can no longer control himself and he eventually urinates on himself. The mother is terribly angry about the fact that the boy has ruined his new suit, and Trina gets embarrassed and tries to avoid the whole situation. McTeague asks her, "What—what is the matter?" Trina does not answer: "Trina's face was scarlet. 'Nothing, nothing,' she exclaimed hastily, looking away" (86). This is the background from which Trina emerges.

Moreover, the family's inability to think beyond their bodily functions is a factor that impedes their integration into the progressive industrial society. Warren French notes that while civilization is advancing, characters like Trina's father are disintegrating due to their focus on bodily functions and their lack of understanding of the new, mechanized, civilized society. He cites the example of Trina's father and his inability to operate a mechanical toy boat, and believes that this "results in the toy's sinking on its trial run and foreshadows what will happen to the family when he matches wits with the mechanized civilization that produced the boat" (67).

Being the daughter of this family, Trina knows and understands their environment and wants a means of escape from her family. Ironically, to be able to escape from her family, she does have to rely on a bodily function—sexuality. Trina is in need of a relationship. She has two options, two victims which she has captivated being the femme fatale that she is: Marcus Schouler and McTeague. Although the two men are friends, they are distinctly different. In chapter 1, Norris makes the reader aware of the vast differences between Marcus and McTeague. Marcus, who is also her cousin, is introduced at the beginning of the novel as a man who thinks, or claims that he thinks, and is concerned about current social and political issues:

> He was continually making use of the stock phrases of the professional politicians—phrases he had caught at some of the ward "rallies" and "ratification meetings." These rolled off his tongue with incredible emphasis, appearing at every turn of the conversation—"outraged constituencies," "cause of labor," "wage earners," "opinions biased by personal interest," "eyes blinded by party prejudice." (14)

McTeague, on the other hand, is "immensely strong, stupid, docile, obedient" (7). Having these two men as possible suitors,

Trina chooses McTeague. Marcus, who appears to think, does not feel. McTeague, on the other hand, appears to feel but does not in any way think. Her choice is devious. McTeague is able to satisfy her desire to have a sexual relationship, he is able to provide her with a new home, and most important, he is easily controlled and dominated because of his stupidity. Moreover, if Trina chooses to marry Marcus, because he is related to her by blood, she will not be able to rid herself of the roots of her family. She will create for herself another tangled mesh of inherited family traits, and she will not be able to escape from her family. McTeague is Trina's perfect victim and Trina's perfect means of escape. The femme fatale is in full command once she has McTeague entrapped in her web.

The idea of entrapment and entanglement is reiterated several times during the course of McTeague and Trina's engagement. Norris uses words such as "charming," "penetrating," "delicious," "dazzling," "delicate," "sweet," and "enervating," to describe the effects this femme fatale has on McTeague and to suggest Trina's association with enchantress figures (25–26). Once McTeague is introduced to all these effects, he can no longer control his instincts. Trina, the femme fatale, acts as a catalyst that brings out all the sexual and animalistic instincts that are present in McTeague. She has ensured herself of McTeague's blind submission to her and, consequently, she has ensured herself of a new home.

After making her choice, and during the engagement period, Norris constantly reminds the reader of the danger and threats this femme fatale poses to McTeague. After spending an entire day with the Sieppes on a picnic, it is decided that Marcus and McTeague will spend the night with the family. After much deliberation, it is decided that McTeague is to sleep in Trina's room. Once he finds himself in her own room and among her personal belongings, McTeague is captivated. He forgets how Trina had looked on that particular day and he only remembers the image of the femme fatale, the image Trina left on him the first time they met:

> He had but to close his eyes to see her as distinctly as in a mirror. He saw her tiny, round figure, dressed all in black—for, curiously enough, it was his very first impression of Trina that came back to him now—not the Trina of the later occasions, not the Trina of the blue-cloth skirt and white sailor. He saw her as he had seen her the day that Marcus had introduced them; saw her pale, round face; her narrow, half-open eyes, blue like the eyes of a baby; her tiny pale ears, suggestive of anemia; the freckles across the bridge of her nose; her pale lips; the tiara of royal black hair; and above all, the delicious poise of the head...(65)

And on their wedding night, the same image is reiterated:

> The dentist saw again, as if for the first time, her small, pale face looking out from beneath her royal tiara of black hair; he saw again her long, narrow blue eyes; her lips, nose, and tiny ears, pale and bloodless and suggestive of anemia...(127)

The images that McTeague keeps seeing serve the function of emphasizing the presence of the femme fatale and also serve the function of emphasizing the full control she has over her defenseless prey, McTeague. Pizer analyzes McTeague's degeneration on the basis of his inherited animalistic traits. Pizer believes, "McTeague's fall is the product of both his special circumstance as an atavistic criminal and his general sensual fallibility as a man. Both flaws stress man's atavistic nature, that he is frequently controlled by unanalyzable instincts which derive from his family and racial past" (*The Novels of Frank* 62). I do agree with Pizer on the fact that McTeague's inherited traits lead to his ultimate ruin, yet I also stress the role the femme fatale has in bringing out these inherited traits. Moreover, Pizer fails to notice the psychological effects this femme fatale is producing on her victim. McTeague, who is extremely stupid and shallow, is having to deal with these images of Trina that keep recurring. Why is McTeague, who can never think beyond his bodily functions, captivated by this woman? The answer lies in the fact that Trina is a femme fatale. French notices the effects that this particular woman has on her victim and compares the fall of McTeague to the fall of man. He describes Trina as a "serpent" and asserts "the stage is set for the hero's eventual downfall" (65). Locked into a trap, McTeague is regarded as a "hero" who will eventually be crushed because of his encounter with the seductress.

The melancholic wail that McTeague keeps singing to himself serves as another indication that McTeague does, in fact, have feelings and is under the spell of the seductress who is luring him into a trap: "No one to love, none to caress. Left all alone in this world's wilderness" (53). The song foreshadows the events to come, and it also informs the reader of McTeague's need for more than a sexual relationship. McTeague is, after all, a human being despite the fact that he is repeatedly described as a brute. There are hints for the reader to decipher—McTeague needs love and affection; Trina is deadly and cannot meet his emotional needs.

In one of his early encounters with Trina, McTeague struggles to rid himself of his atavism. Although Pizer believes "the struggle between flesh and spirit does not occur within McTeague" in the instance when McTeague kisses Trina when she is anesthetized (*The Novels of Frank* 61), I tend to believe that it does occur:

> Why could he not always love her purely, cleanly? What was this perverse, vicious thing that lived within him, knitted to his flesh?
> Below the fine fabric of all that was good in him ran the foul stream of hereditary evil, like a sewer. The vices and sins of his father and of his father's father, to the third and fourth and five hundredth generation tainted him. The evil of an entire race flowed in his veins. Why should it be? He did not desire it. Was he to blame? (Norris 29)

The answer to McTeague's question is no. Trina acts as a catalyst for bringing out all of his brutality. It is true that given McTeague's hereditary disposition toward atavism, the victory of the brute is beyond his control, yet to blame his brutality solely on his atavism is to disregard the effect Trina has on McTeague. McTeague is struggling under the influence of Trina and is hoping to find a way for the spirit to overcome the flesh. In the process of wooing Trina and getting her to accept his proposal, his bodily urges are in full control. After the marriage takes place, and once his bodily urges are satisfied, Trina acts as a civilizing influence on McTeague and produces a better version of McTeague. The fact that she is able to civilize McTeague indicates that McTeague can be molded and shaped into a good person, a person who can now give way to the spirit as well as the flesh. This is another aspect to look into with regard to the femme fatale. Why does Trina bring out all of his brutality in the beginning, and then why does she decide to better his life and improve his daily habits?

The answer lies in the fact that she, herself, has many inherited traits of which she is trying to rid herself. She chooses McTeague because of her need for a sexual relationship and other reasons as well. But once she chooses McTeague, she realizes that it is time she try to rid herself of her background and the family traits that she has inherited.

During the time of their engagement, Trina is kind and generous to some extent. None of her inherited traits seems to rise to the surface yet. She makes sure that McTeague gets the "one unsatisfied longing" of having the big gold tooth for a sign (105). After having a fight with Marcus about Trina, McTeague returns to his apartment and finds a package addressed to him, and to his surprise, "it was the tooth—the famous golden molar with its huge prongs—his sign, his ambition, the one unrealized dream of his life" (116). According to Pizer, this sign "represents his pride in his profession, and in a large sense it symbolizes for him the dental profession as a whole" (*The Novels of Frank* 76). By giving him this sign as a present, Trina is trying to manage and control one of the most valuable things in his life—his profession.

Unlike her mother, Mrs. Sieppe, who is very dry and unloving toward her entire family, Trina, at the beginning of her marriage to McTeague, tries to be otherwise. She appears to be a very loving wife. She loves McTeague and needs to be loved in return: "Oh Mac, do you truly love, really love me—love me big?" (108). She carries out her full responsibilities as a wife, not only in cooking, cleaning, and doing the household chores, but also in providing love and support to her husband.

Another manipulating course of action Trina takes as a femme fatale in their marriage is the changes that she is able to make in McTeague: "Instead of sinking to McTeague's level as she had feared, Trina found that she could make McTeague rise to hers, and in this saw a solution of many a difficult and gloomy complication" (147).

All of these loving gestures take place because Trina is trying to get rid of her inherited traits. She does not want to be as cold as her mother, and she also does not want to be as miserly as her ancestors. In the process, McTeague is being shaped into a human being who has the potential to surmount his bodily urges and pave the way for the spirit to play a role in his life.

Trina Wins the Lottery

The turning point from which Trina can no longer control heredity and environment takes place when Trina wins the lottery. One of the basic tenets of American naturalism is the idea of fate and what takes place because of man's predestined fate. Commenting on Frank Norris' treatment of the problem of free will, Ahnebrink suggests that Norris "showed man devoid of free will, helpless in the face of biological and social forces, or a victim of fate" (194). Ahnebrink adds that in *McTeague*, "fate played a certain role in the lives of the characters and contributed to their downfall" (197). In the case of McTeague, fate predestines him to meet the femme fatale, Trina. In the case of Trina, fate predestines her to win the lottery as she is planning to marry McTeague: "Chance had brought them face to face, and mysterious instincts as ungovernable as the winds of heaven were at work knitting their lives together" (74). Both become victims of their predestined fate, and neither has control over what will become of their lives.

When Trina wins the lottery, her greed and love of money emerge. She strives to overcome this problem in many ways. She decides to buy kitchen utensils and other necessities for her new home by setting aside $200 for that, she buys McTeague the golden tooth, and she even decides not to keep the money in her own possession and, therefore, invests it in her rich Uncle Oelbermann's business. Yet, Norris sets forth a warning:

> It soon became apparent that Trina would be an extraordinarily good housekeeper. Economy was her strong point.

A good deal of peasant blood still ran undiluted in her veins, and she had all the instinct of a hardy and penurious mountain race—the instinct which saves without any thought, without idea of consequence, saving for the sake of saving, hoarding without knowing why. (107)

Trina, who has victimized McTeague and entrapped him within her web, is now entangled in a web of her own. She, who has cleverly chosen McTeague as her husband, now has a problem of her own to deal with. She becomes entangled in her love for money and her unexplainable greed. She cannot control fate, which has predestined her to win the lottery. Similarly, McTeague cannot control fate, which has predestined him to encounter the femme fatale. Fate is at its fullest force, working upon these two characters, bringing them to their destructive ends.

Trina fails at overcoming her greed: "It was a passion with her to save money" (148). Three years of blissful marriage elapse, and then Trina and McTeague have their first quarrel about renting a house. Trina starts to realize that she is controlled by the stronger force of her inherited love of money. She keeps thinking and worrying about her problem: "I didn't use to be so stingy...Since I won the lottery I've become a regular little miser. It's growing on me...and anyhow, I can't help it" (164).

In an attempt to overcome her problem with greed, Trina tries to gain more control over McTeague. She shapes him gradually into a modified version of himself: "Gradually the dentist improved under the influence of his little wife...He read the newspapers; he subscribed to a dental magazine; on Easter, Christmas, and New Year's he went to church with Trina" (150–151). Sexually, she is in full command of their marital relationship: "On occasions they sat like this for an hour or so, philandering, Trina cuddling herself down upon McTeague's enormous body, rubbing her cheek against the grain of his unshaven chin, kissing the bald spot on the top of his head, or putting her fingers into his ears and eyes" (196). However, once her problem is out of control, and when McTeague loses his dentistry practice, she not only tries to control him sexually and intellectually, but she tries to control him financially as well. When McTeague loses his job, Trina becomes obsessed with saving money. This is the turning point for McTeague when he finally decides to take action against his manipulative, dominating, and destructive wife.

In *Frank Norris Revisited*, Joseph McElrath, Jr., points out, "*McTeague* concerns the rise and fall of an individual." McElrath holds Trina responsible for the rise of McTeague:

> McTeague is a success story for half of its length, as the hero experiences upward mobility, transcending the limitations of both his low intelligence and humble origins. Because of the aid of a wife given to impeccable housekeeping and financial management, his own dutiful performance in his largely self-taught profession of dentistry, and the extraordinary good fortune of Mrs. McTeague having won $5,000 in a lottery, he has come to taste the pleasures of American life not known to his parents. (36)

McElrath, however, does not hold Trina fully responsible for the downfall of McTeague. He believes that several factors cause this downfall. These factors include Marcus' need for revenge by reporting McTeague to the authorities for practicing dentistry without a license, the fact that Trina and McTeague move into poorer quarters, and the fact that Trina does not share the cost of McTeague's loss of the $35 dollars he put into their projected house, are the contributors that bring about McTeague's downfall, resulting in a "downward movement" of McTeague (46–47). Seen from this perspective, the naturalistic world of determinism is in full command of McTeague. It is my belief, however, that McTeague is aware of the threat that Trina poses to his life. He comes to the realization that Trina has been using and abusing him for her own purposes of saving money. In one of his angry moments, McTeague asks, "Are you my boss, I'd like to know? Who's the boss, you or I?" Trina replies by asking him a question in return: "Who's got the money, I'd like to know?" (211). From this point on, we watch McTeague taking action against Trina, reverting to his motto, "You can't make small of me" (78). He becomes abusive in their relationship. He then takes all the money she has in her possession in the house and leaves. He later returns to ask for more money, and upon learning that Trina has taken the $5,000 that she has previously kept with her uncle, he finally kills her to get the money. The scene in which McTeague kills Trina is horrific:

> Beside herself with terror, Trina turned and fought him back, fought for her miserable life with the exasperation and strength of a harassed cat and with such energy and such wild, unnatural force that even McTeague for the moment drew back from her. But her resistance was the one thing to drive him to the top of his fury. He came back at her again, his eyes drawn to two fine twinkling points and his enormous fists, clenched till the knuckles whitened, raised in the air.
> Then it became abominable.
> In the schoolroom outside, behind the coal scuttle, the cat listened to the sounds of stamping and struggling and the muffled noise of blows...(288)

Ironically, she is murdered by the man she has captivated, changed, cultivated, and molded, but she is also murdered by the man she has destroyed.

The two subplots that Norris includes within the novel foreshadow the fate of the femme fatale. The first subplot involves

Old Grannis and Miss Baker, who, despite the fact that both are in their 60s, fall in love. Old Grannis and Miss Baker are both shy and reluctant to reveal their love for each other. They spend their time waiting for each other, listening to each other, and sharing experiences with each other. They do all of this through a wall that separates the two lodgers. Gradually, the two lonely people overcome their shyness and communicate with each other in the climactic scene in which Miss Baker offers Old Grannis a cup of tea. The second subplot involves Maria Macapa and Zerkow's affair. Maria is the maid who cleans the building in which McTeague lives, and Zerkow is the Jewish junkman who is fascinated not by Maria but by her story about her ancestors who used to have gold plates. Zerkow and Maria get married and have a child who dies immediately after it is born. Zerkow becomes obsessed with the story of the gold plates and eventually murders Maria because he believes that she is hiding the gold plates from him.

The two subplots offer two alternative paths from which Trina can choose. The first path, Miss Baker's path, is the path that Trina almost begins to follow in her relationship with McTeague. This is the path that can lead to her happiness and produce a fruitful love story. Trina begins by taking this path. She is shy with McTeague, reluctant, and in love with him in the beginning. The subplot offers a moral and benevolent view of love and marriage. The most important aspect of this subplot is its asexuality. The couple's relationship will be a success because of their lack of focus on their sexual instincts. Pizer asserts, "[B]ecause their subplot contains the only successful love match in the novel, Norris seems to be saying that love must be asexual if it is to have the virtues of restraint, generosity, and kindness" (*The Novels of Frank* 74). Furthermore, McElrath believes, "this subplot is satirically fashioned as a counterpart to the more realistic, decidedly anti-Victorian main plot in which not only sexual but other drives loom" (47). The relationship between Trina and McTeague does not follow this model and is, therefore, doomed to failure.

Because Trina is a femme fatale, she chooses to rely on her sexuality in her relationship. She awakens the sexual beast in McTeague and reassures herself of his blind submission to his sexual beast and consequently to herself. Similarly, Maria Macapa awakens the beast in Zerkow by telling and retelling the story of the gold plates. According to McElrath, Zerkow, whose "hereditary acquisitiveness has already been exaggerated to monstrously monomaniacal proportions in his feverish obsession with gold," resembles McTeague in his hereditary brutality and his heavy reliance on his animalistic instincts (48). Both Trina and Maria act as disastrous forces who bring out the beasts in these two men. At one point in the novel, the two women take pride in the sadistic nature they have been able to produce in their husbands, boasting of which one suffers more injury: "They told each other of their husbands' brutalities, taking a strange sort of pride in recounting some particularly savage blow, each trying to make out that her own husband was the most cruel" (240). Zerkow, who in chapter 16, cuts Maria's throat for having forgotten the story of the gold service and thus having "stolen" it from him, foreshadows McTeague's descent to the level of a murderer. Both Trina and Maria act as degenerative forces that bring out the murderers in their husbands, and unfortunately, bring about their own ends. This is the path that Trina chooses.

The construction of the femme fatale becomes complete when Norris chooses not to endow this marital relationship with a child. Trina carries a significant femme fatale characteristic that cannot be overlooked—Trina's inability to conceive and consequently her inability to become a mother. There is only one mention in the novel about the possibility of having a child. This takes place before the wedding as Trina is waiting anxiously to receive her wedding gift from her rich uncle. The gift is "a box of all sorts of toys." Given the limitations of McTeague's thinking, he does not understand the implications: "Why should he send us toys?" he asks Trina. Trina, at this instant, "dropped into a chair and laughed till she cried behind her handkerchief" (126). There is no further mention of any possibility of Trina becoming pregnant. This, in my opinion, is another indication that Norris was creating a femme fatale as he was creating the character of Trina.

In addition to the fact that Trina's creation as a femme fatale may account for the absence of children in her life, it might also be useful to take a look at families from a historical point of view. Toward the end of the nineteenth century, the family was an unstable institution both from within its own boundaries and society at large. According to Priscilla Clement, "for some children in the late-nineteenth-century city, family ties were entirely dissolved. Parents died or deserted these youngsters or simply could not afford to support them. Such children created a real and visible problem" (251). At the turn of the twentieth century, many child-saving movements were created to improve the situations of broken and inadequate families' health, delinquency, morality, poverty, schooling, dependency and neglect, discrimination and early child development (Cohen 274).

These may be factors that Norris took into consideration while writing *McTeague*, but there are other factors that underlie the absence of a potential offspring of McTeague and Trina. Because both Trina and McTeague are in desperate need for a sexual relationship, emotion does not play a part in their marriage. McTeague has a new bodily urge to master—sexuality; Trina is preoccupied with thoughts on money. Pizer believes that Trina's miserliness runs parallel with McTeague's atavism, and therefore, because both of them are "caught up by drives and instincts beyond their control or comprehension, they mate by chance rather than by will" (*The Novels of Frank* 72). As a result, their mating is fruitless.

As the novel progresses, we witness Trina, the femme fatale, who is controlled by her love of money, perform sexual acts with the golden coins instead of with her husband:

> She would draw the heap [of money] lovingly toward her and bury her face in it, delighted at the smell of it and the feel of the smooth, cool metal on her cheeks. She even put the smaller gold pieces in her mouth and jingled them there. She loved her money with an intensity that she could hardly express. She would plunge her small fingers into the pile with little murmurs of affection, her long narrow eyes half closed and shining, her breath coming in long sighs. (238)

This famous passage from the novel has been read in the context of Trina's sexual impulses and urges which have to be satisfied. On the other hand, the sexual acts that Trina performs with her money can also be read as maternal acts and as an appeal for Trina for wanting to be a mother; yet given the circumstances that she has been created as a femme fatale, she cannot bear the responsibilities that come along with having children. Acts such as burying her face in the money, smelling it, feeling its smoothness, and loving it with intensity are all acts that a nurturing mother performs with her baby. Trina is deprived of having a baby because she is a femme fatale; therefore, she performs these acts as a way of compensating for the motherhood of which she has been deprived.

In preparing his plot summary for *McTeague*, it is interesting to note that Norris' original plan for Trina was for her to be a kindergarten teacher. Norris writes, "McTeague, who is a third-class dentist in an uptown business street, marries Trina, a kindergarten teacher" (Pizer, *The Novels of Frank* 53). Norris later changed his original plan and placed her in a position that still involves children but with no direct contact with children. She is a maker of ark animals. As she explains her work to McTeague, Norris makes the reader aware of the fact that this woman will not bear children:

> She made Noah's ark animals, whittling them out of a block of soft wood with a sharp jackknife, the only instrument she used. Trina was very proud to explain her work to McTeague as he had already explained his own to her. "They sell for nine cents a dozen. Only I can't make the manikins."
> "The manikins?"
> "The little figures you know—Noah and his wife, and Shem, and all the others."
> It was true. Trina could not whittle them fast enough and cheap enough to compete with the turning lathe, that could throw off whole tribes and peoples of manikins while she was fashioning one family. Everything else, however, she made—the ark itself, all windows and no door...(107)

Due to the reproductive incapacity of Trina as a femme fatale, even her profession reflects the fact that she cannot conceive and bear children. The image of Trina producing animals instead of people and the image of Trina's arks that are "all windows and no door" predict the effects that this femme fatale will have on her male victim. She eventually brings out the destructive animal in McTeague, and she finds herself crushed in the end, without a door through which she can escape from the animal of her creation.

Furthermore, toward the end of the novel and after Trina's fingers had been amputated, "Trina became a scrubwoman. She had taken council of Selina [her cousin], and through her had obtained the position of caretaker in a little memorial kindergarten over on Pacific Street" (271). For the second time, Norris places Trina in a position that does not involve direct contact with children, but does, nevertheless, involve children. By doing so, it is my opinion that Norris is emphasizing the fact that Trina, as a femme fatale, should not and cannot perform the tasks of a nurturing woman who can get involved in children's lives. The construction of the femme fatale becomes complete once Norris adds the element of the absence of children in the life of this woman.

Having established that Trina is a dangerous woman, it remains to speak about the various interpretations literary critics have given to the fall of McTeague and Trina. There is one explanation that justifies why McTeague eventually murders Trina— that of his inherited brutality that rises to the surface under the effects of alcohol along with mistreatment. McTeague, despite his stupidity and grotesqueness, is a gentle person: "There was nothing vicious about the man" (7). He has, however, been victimized by the femme fatale, and this leads him to his tragic fall. He has lived peacefully until he encounters Trina. His world consists of working in his dental parlor and watching the daily events that take place on Polk Street. McTeague's life is one of constant repetition in an ordered world. Trina disrupts the routine and turns his world topsy-turvy. After their marriage, for a short time, she manages to bring stability back into his life. She is a good housekeeper, and she introduces him to a higher level of living. In other words, she tames him. However, when McTeague loses his profession, his world starts to crumble, and along with the increasing miserliness of his wife, McTeague reverts to the brute in him—the brute who is "so close to the surface" (27). Her taming of McTeague is only temporary. She does not manage to bring a permanent change in McTeague because she cannot make a permanent change in herself.

Trina, on the other hand, is murdered because she is a femme fatale who victimizes McTeague. She shrewdly chooses McTeague as a husband. After their marriage takes places, and while in the process of taming McTeague, she is struggling to get rid of her own inherited traits. She struggles to rid McTeague of his gross habits and is always afraid "she would...come to be like him, would sink to the level of steam beer and cheap tobacco, and all her pretty ways, her clean, trim little habits, would be forgotten, since they would be thrown away upon her stupid, brutish husband" (146). She manages, nevertheless, to upgrade the level of McTeague's life style. However, her own inherited traits rise unimpeded to the surface, and she finds herself fighting two battles in the household instead of one. Not only is she faced with the difficult task of molding her husband, she is also facing the difficult task of fighting against her love of money and her stingy habits. Once she gives in to her love of money, she begins to lose both battles.

There are various interpretations for Trina's self-destructive greed. Pizer offers an insightful interpretation and claims, "[T]he theme of *McTeague* is not that greed and drunkenness lead to a tragic fall, but that tragedy is inherent in the human situation given man's animal past and the possibility that he will be dominated by that past in particular circumstances" (*The Novels of Frank* 84). Moreover, Pizer stresses, "[T]he uncontrollable power of the past" and argues, "man's individual family heritage combines as a force toward reversion—that is toward a return to the emotions and instincts of his animal past—which under propitious circumstances controls and dominates him" (*The Novels of Frank* 64). Pizer's explanation of the past and its power over the individual justifies why Trina is transformed from a trim, orderly housekeeper into a driven, ravaged, obsessive miser.

Barbara Hochman, in her article, "Loss, Habit, Obsession: The Governing Dynamic of *McTeague*," offers a different perspective as to why Trina's greed becomes a critical problem and eventually causes her murder. Hochman believes *McTeague* is animated not by the desperate lust for gain, but rather by "the haunting fear of loss, to which greed is but one response" (179). In the case of Trina, Hochman argues, "Trina's terror of loss of self should be conceptualized in terms of loss of habits" (185). According to Hochman, Trina feels violated at the sexual level after she surrenders to McTeague on their wedding night: "[F]or Trina, sexual surrender means surrender and submission of many kinds, culminating in her feeling that she has lost control, and, therefore, lost herself." Taking vengeance for losing herself, Hochman believes, "[I]t is for this reason that she later guards her money" (185).

In *Frank Norris: Instinct and Art*, William B. Dillingham justifies Trina's love of money and argues that Trina, like McTeague, is the victim of heredity:

> When Trina decides her greed is too strong for her to fight, it slowly begins to consume her. It draws her away from McTeague and the life she previously led. Ultimately, it brings her to near-madness and then to death at the hands of her husband, whose degenerate mind is angered by her greed. (75)

All of these critics offer insightful explanations of Trina's transformation from a good housekeeper and loving wife to an obsessive, stingy miser. It is my opinion, however, that Norris creates a femme fatale in Trina, and, based on this fact, I will offer my own explanation as to why Trina is eventually crushed.

Trina needs a means of escape from the family she lives with, a family that is totally controlled by heredity. Upon meeting McTeague, she realizes that he can easily be wrapped around her finger. In that way, she rescues herself from the controlling environment she lives in and in turn takes control of her new household, including taking control of her victim, McTeague. Matters are in her hand until Trina wins the lottery. Unfortunately, she no longer has control over her hereditary traits or her husband, and is murdered by her victim. With the murder of Trina, the cycle of victimization comes to an end: She, the victim of her controlling environment, becomes the victimizer of McTeague; McTeague, once her victim, becomes the victimizer who puts an end to the whole process of victimization. The femme fatale is killed by the man she has entrapped. Ernest Marchand brilliantly exposes the idea of entrapment in his analysis of the conversation that takes place between Trina and Mrs. Sieppe as Trina is explaining to her mother what has happened at the B Station between her and McTeague:

> Trina burst in upon her mother while the latter was setting a mousetrap in the kitchen.
> "Oh mamma!"
> "Eh, Trina? Ach, what has happun?"
> Trina told her in a breath.
> "Soh soon?" was Mrs. Sieppe's first comment. "Eh, well, what you cry for, then?"
> "I don't know," wailed Trina, plucking at the end of her handkerchief.
> "You loaf der younge doctor?"
> "I don't know."...
> "You don' know, you don' know? Where haf your senses gone, Trina? You kiss der doctor. You cry, and you don' know..."

Mrs. Sieppe set down the mousetrap with such violence
that it sprung with a sharp snap. (71)

Marchand believes, "[T]he chapter ends, with the trap a symbol
of Trina's marriage" (40). Although Marchand may seem to be
implying that Trina is the one who will be entrapped in this marriage, I argue that it is McTeague who in fact is the "mouse" that
will be "snapped" in the marriage.

The idea of animals being trapped is reiterated in the canary in
its golden cage that is always with McTeague, even in Death Valley. McTeague is affiliated with this canary and treats the canary
with utmost care. According to Warren French, McTeague's deep
attachment to the bird serves to show the reader that McTeague
does in fact have a good heart that might have triumphed had
it not been distracted by the glitter of golden coins (70). It also
serves to show an animal captured and victimized the way
McTeague has been captured and victimized. Both of these factors account for McTeague's strong attachment to the bird.

The stages that Ahnebrink outlines of the love and the marriage of McTeague and Trina are the stages that are expected
from a relationship between a femme fatale and her lover:

> In the lives of McTeague and Trina "love" spelled a curse,
> for the "mysterious instincts" that bound them irrevo-
> cably together ultimately caused their destruction. The
> stages of McTeague's "love" of Trina went from brutal
> desire, to gratification of desire, satiety, indifference, cru-
> elty, sadism, and finally, murder. (211)

In this naturalistic novel, circumstances will that McTeague
comes under the influence of the femme fatale. Trina at first may
call for the reader's sympathy as she is entrapped in a controlling

world. We, as readers, are satisfied to see that she is able to escape her parental world. We also admire the fact that she tries to bring about positive changes in McTeague. However, Trina loses our sympathy once she can no longer fight her inherited traits and gives in to her love of money. At the same time, we start to feel compassion and sympathy for McTeague, who falls under the spell of this femme fatale.

Chapter 3

"I am Yours Truly:" Caroline Meeber as Femme Fatale in Theodore Dreiser's *Sister Carrie*

Although the title of Theodore Dreiser's novel suggests the presence of a nun, Caroline Meeber in *Sister Carrie* is, in fact, another embodiment of the femme fatale in American naturalistic writings. Caroline Meeber's heredity and environment create her as a femme fatale. Unlike Trina, who is influenced more by heredity than by the immediate environment, Sister Carrie is influenced more by the environment than her heredity.

Her heredity and background, nevertheless, do play a role in her transformation into a femme fatale. Sister Carrie is not born with the characteristics of the femme fatale, especially the physical characteristics, but rather she is created as a femme fatale through the surrounding environment of the big city in which she finds herself. This chapter traces Carrie's transformation into a femme fatale as a result of the events that take place when Carrie first arrives to Chicago and investigates whether or not Carrie is strong enough to overcome heredity and environment. Through an analysis of the events that gradually mold Carrie into a femme fatale figure, the chapter traces the trajectory of the rise and fall of the femme fatale. The chapter also examines her relationships with Charles Drouet, George Hurstwood, and Bob Ames and explains the role that each one of these men plays in the life of the femme fatale. The chapter discusses the ending of the novel and concludes with a comparison between Trina and Sister Carrie.

THE FORMULATION OF THE FEMME FATALE

Carrie does not come to the big city with the realization of the power that she has as a beautiful young woman. She comes with pure intentions, motivated by a strong urge to find a job. However, from the beginning of the novel, Dreiser points out that Carrie comes from a poor background:

> When Caroline Meeber boarded the afternoon train for Chicago, her total outfit consisted of a small trunk, a cheap imitation alligator-skin satchel, a small lunch in a paperbox, and a yellow leather snap purse, containing her ticket, a scrap of paper with her sister's address in Van Buren Street, and [$4] in money (7)

At the same time, Dreiser stresses her innocence: "She was [18] years of age, bright, timid, and full of the illusions of ignorance and youth" (7). The image of Carrie boarding the train is a typical naturalistic image in which free will and determinism are para-doxically intertwined. Her poor background is from what she is trying to escape. The cheap luggage and the cheap alligator skin satchel are signs of her family's poverty. By getting on the train to Chicago, Carrie is guided by her free will, and she believes that going to the big city is an opportunity for her to escape. According to Lars Ahnebrink, in naturalistic writings, "[M]an can be explained in terms of heredity and environment which operate upon him" (vii). Ahnebrink's theory can be applied to Sister Carrie, and one can argue that in *Sister Carrie*, Dreiser mentions Carrie's past and her family's poverty. However, Drei-ser does not dwell on Carrie's past because, in Carrie's situa-tion, it is the environment which will have the more significant effect in creating this femme fatale. Therefore, Dreiser warns the reader of the effects that the environment will have on Car-rie: "When a girl leaves her home at [18], she does one of two things. Either she falls into saving hands and becomes better, or she rapidly assumes the cosmopolitan standard of virtue and becomes worse" (7).

Carrie, who is "possessed of a mind rudimentary in its power of observation and analysis," is headed toward the big city. Motivated by "self-interest" and "quick to understand the keener pleasures of life," Carrie has her mind set on material gain (8). Because she comes from a poor background, Carrie sees this as an opportunity to make money and enjoy her life as a young woman. While she is on the train, Charles Drouet is instantly attracted to her. Although Carrie, in the beginning of the novel, does not possess the exceptional physical beauty of the femme fatale, men are, nevertheless, easily attracted to her youth and innocence: "He [Drouet] recognized the indescribable thing that made up for fascination and beauty in her" (11). While Drouet casually makes conversation with Carrie, she herself has her own interest in him as she admires his shoes, suit, and, most important, the "roll of green backs" in his purse (12). Seeing this, she gives Drouet her sister's address and gives him permission to call on her while she is staying there.

From the onset of the novel, the reader is made aware that, despite her youth and inexperience, Carrie knows and understands the social and moral conventions of her time, yet she chooses to transgress. As the train approaches Chicago, Carrie warns Drouet not to resume talking to her once she meets her sister. She realizes that she should not have spoken to Drouet on the train, but she does so despite that. Once she meets her sister, "she felt cold reality taking her by the hand," waking her from the merry dreams she has just had by conversing with Drouet (15). It is made clear from the moment Carrie meets her sister, Mrs. Hanson, that family ties in Carrie's family are dissolved, and that Carrie will not stay for long with her sister because of her encounter with Drouet. Her future in her sister's household does not look promising: "When he [Drouet] disappeared she felt his absence thoroughly. With her sister, she was much alone, a lone figure in a tossing, thoughtless sea" (15).

Carrie begins her new, desolate life in her sister's household. The apartment is dismal and her brother-in-law is offensive and unwelcoming. She understands that she must find work immediately to pay for her room and board. Her dreams of the big city and the possibilities that it offers are instantaneously shattered both from inside her sister's household and outside the household as she starts to look for employment. Inside her sister's house, "she felt the drag of a lean and narrow life," and she notices the changes in her sister after being married to Mr. Hanson: "She was now a thin, though rugged, woman of twenty-seven, with ideas of life colored by her husband's" (19).

Carrie, who is bright, imaginative, and full of energy, stands in sharp contrast with her sister Minnie and Minnie's husband. Carrie realizes that she is caught in another web of a deterministic world. She escapes from her family's poverty only to find herself in another poor, lifeless atmosphere. In *Theodore Dreiser: His World and His Novels*, Richard Lehan comments on Minnie and Hanson's way of life as "dull, plodding, lifeless, caught in a meaningless and empty routine, dead before they are in the grave" (69). This lifestyle does not suit the young and ambitious Carrie. She must find employment not only as a means of paying for her stay there, but also as a means of escaping from this household. Thus, Carrie begins her laborious search. Frightened, Carrie moves from one manufacturing house to another and from one department store to another, only to be rejected immediately. Eventually, she is able to get a job in a shoe factory at $4.50 a week.

Despite Carrie's satisfaction at being able to finally find a job, she finds herself facing yet another struggle. She finds the city incomprehensible and mysterious. Moreover, she begins to realize that she is caught in an industrial, capitalist, merciless world—a world that does not match the dreamland she had envisioned and does not promise to fulfill all the dreams she has had upon her arrival to the city. Ahnebrink provides an accurate explanation of the effects of industrialism and the rise of the city upon individuals such as Carrie who live in a naturalistic world:

> The effects of industrialism were many and far-reaching. Among other things it gave rise to a new hierarchy of financial giants and at the same time it created an industrial

proletariat made up of individuals who were mere cogs in a machine, insignificant beings subjected to a standardized order. (2)

A sequence of disappointments, therefore, is giving birth to the femme fatale in Sister Carrie: her poverty-stricken life with her family on a farm in Wisconsin, her new life with her sister in a "narrow humdrum place" (36), and her new job where "the whole atmosphere was sordid" (42). The whole city is not what she envisioned. All of these factors are paving the way for Carrie to decide to use her sexuality as a means of attaining what her heart desires most—money. She begins as an innocent young woman who decides to come into the big city to make a living, yet all of these deterministic factors are playing a part in the formulation of Carrie as a femme fatale. Her free will comes into play when she decides to break free from these determining factors. Her encounters with Drouet, first on the train and later as she is walking in the streets of Chicago, hungry, lonely, and seeking employment, are acts of fate in a naturalistic world which she cleverly makes use of to her own personal advantage and gain.

In addition to the disappointments that Carrie is facing, and despite her lack of money, Carrie finds herself being pulled strongly toward the fashionable world that the big city encompasses. The department stores have been recently created with the specific task of targeting young women. The "advertising craze" that took place in the 1880s had flourished and envisioned women as their main consumers (Leob 5). While Carrie is desperately in search for a job, she cannot resist the temptation of looking into the grand department stores, although she knows that she cannot even afford to look. Carrie wonders at the array of commodities she is looking at in the department stores as the commodities are laid out elegantly to attract women to buy them. Thus, we find Carrie wondering how she, in her present state, can acquire some of these commodities:

> Carrie passed along the busy aisles, much affected by the remarkable displays of trinkets, dress goods, stationery, and jewelry. Each separate counter was a showplace of dazzling interest and attraction. She could not help feeling the claim of each trinket and valuable upon her personally, and yet she did not stop. There was nothing there which she could not have used—nothing which she did not long to own. (26)

Drouet helps Carrie acquire some of these goods, yet, more importantly, Drouet's main role in the novel is that he is the male character who introduces Carrie to the power she has as a woman. In Dreiser's initial description of Drouet, the reader is made aware of the fact that Drouet will not seek any kind of permanent relationship with Carrie; rather Carrie will be a source of pleasure to him:

> Good clothes, of course, were the first essential, the things without which he was nothing. A strong physical nature, actuated by a keen desire for the feminine was the next. A mind free of any consideration of the problems or forces of the world and actuated not by greed, but an insatiable love of variable pleasure. (10)

When Drouet meets Carrie for the second time in the streets of Chicago, Carrie is at her weakest moment—tired, hungry, unemployed, and helpless. Drouet takes advantage of her situation and invites her to dinner. Impressed by the prices and the atmosphere of the restaurant, Carrie confides in Drouet, and she makes him aware of her frustration and pain. He takes advantage of her desperation and offers her help: "Let me help you. You take some of my money." Carrie, in turn, takes advantage of his offer: "He pressed her hand gently, and she tried to withdraw it. At this, he held it fast, and she no longer protested" (61). She realizes at this instance that she does have power of her own, power which she has never known and has never taken advantage of before—the power of the feminine, the power of beauty, and the power of sexuality. She also realizes that along with this power comes the power of money. The scene ends with Drouet handing her $20: "Carrie left him, feeling as though a great arm had slipped out before her to draw off trouble. The money she had accepted was two soft, green, handsome ten-dollar bills" (62).

Carrie understands the value of money, especially after she has worked and been fired by the shoe factory. With the $20 in her possession, Carrie is left with her thoughts: "Ah money, money, money! What a thing it was to have. How plenty of it would clear away all these troubles" (67). With the thought of money and its power, Carrie is easily convinced by Drouet to leave her sister's household. Dreiser does not go into any specific details of the night that Carrie gives in to Drouet; he does, however, set the scene for that night. Carrie and Drouet go to the theater, where she is fascinated by its spectacle of wealth and magnificence. At the same time, Carrie is troubled by the cold December night and is also disturbed when she catches a glimpse of one of the girls who used to work with her in the shoe factory. After the theater, Carrie and Drouet have dinner at a fine restaurant. Having set this scene:

> Dreiser has captured the nature and intensity of Carrie's emotional life at this moment—the fear which she associates with cold and the factory, the excitement of life represented by the theatre, and her association of Drouet both with this excitement and with a warm refuge from want. (Pizer, *The Novels of Theodore* 86)

Motivated by her love of the things money can buy and do for her, Carrie will from this point on use her femininity and sexuality to attract men and, consequently, not only overcome her fears of living in the city, but also satisfy her own needs of having pretty clothes, shoes, and perfumes—the good things in life.

Literary critics have written extensively about Carrie's exploitation of her feminine attractiveness in order to attain personal gain. W. M. Frohock comments on life in Chicago where "money and commodities are what count," and suggests, "the men that [Carrie] meets teach her that physical attractiveness is a commodity, fully negotiable" (13). Richard Lehan asserts, "Carrie has one thing to sell—and that is her body" (60). She has nothing else to offer to the city and utilizes her body to keep her alive and well. Moreover, John J. McAleer believes, "[Carrie] does appear to barter sex to put herself on the road to better opportunities." McAleer also asserts that Carrie does this "not as an opportunist, however, but one out of force of circumstance" (77). McAleer seems to validate the argument that Carrie is not born as a dangerous woman and does not have the intention of being one until she reaches Chicago and realizes that in order to survive and rise in the city, she has to make use of her body and her sexuality that easily attract men to her. Circumstances are stronger than Carrie, and from the point when she runs away with Drouet, Carrie is trying to take control of the circumstances that she has been facing since she left her home in Wisconsin.

In the process of reversing her helplessness and becoming a strong woman in the face of the harsh circumstances and surrounding environment, Carrie is exploiting the power she has as a woman, and she is also overstepping the moral standards upon which she has been raised. Carrie easily succumbs to Drouet without any moral conflict. Many literary critics agree on the fact that there is no moral conflict taking place within Carrie as she leaves with Drouet. W. M. Frohock maintains that in giving in to Drouet "there is no moral conflict...she just exploits the one commodity she has" (13). James Lundquist argues, "[T]hrough her fall, Carrie has risen, and she will not act the part of the ruined girl" (31), and William Marion Reedy asserts, "[Carrie's] fall is a fall upwards" (157). Furthermore, Philip Gerber in *Theodore Dreiser Revisited* suggests that Carrie "follows the dictates of her sense of self-interest as it leads her—or promises to lead her—toward desired goals. And on this level, her behavior, in the social sense, is decidedly unconventional" (26).

The concept of determinism, which is fundamental in naturalistic writings, accounts for Carrie's behavior and her fall into the hands of men. In *Sister Carrie*, we find the female protagonist oppressed by the society and enslaved by the existing social and economic conditions that surround her, hence the destruction of her belief in moral and ethical values. However, the destruction of her belief in these values does not lead to her own destruction per se. She is not defeated and ruined by society because of the fact that she decides to manipulate the men she encounters. Rigorous determinism exists in her life as a naturalistic character, but as a femme fatale, determinism does not by any means rule her life and does not lead her to her death. Carrie has a will of her own and struggles to triumph over the surrounding environment. Unlike Maggie in Stephen Crane's novella, for example, Carrie makes use of her fall, and instead of undergoing a process of degeneration, she undergoes a process of rising in the world. Carrie is the product of her environment, helpless in the face of social forces, a victim of fate, yet paradoxically, this product of the environment becomes a strong and threatening deadly woman who turns herself into a victimizer of men.

Carrie succumbs to Drouet, but more important, she succumbs to the overpowering appeal of her own beauty and the possibilities she can attain: "Carrie's new state was remarkable in that she saw possibilities in it" (75); "she looked into her glass and saw a prettier Carrie than she had seen before," and she finds herself "established in a pleasant fashion, free of certain difficulties which most ominously confronted her" (91). Thus, it is Charles Drouet who plays a significant role in the creation of the femme fatale. Pizer sees Drouet as the seducer of Carrie, who is innocent at that time, and maintains that Carrie's story is "that of the innocent young girl from the country who is seduced by the city villain" (*The Novels of Theodore* 37).

The Femme Fatale in Full Action
Carrie comes to the full realization of the power she has once she is introduced to George Hurstwood. Carrie is perfectly content with Drouet until she meets Hurstwood and sees an even better means of escape than Drouet. Hurstwood, who is introduced early in the novel as the manager of Fitzgerald and Moy, one of the famous and frequented saloons in Chicago, is to play a significant role in showing what the femme fatale is capable of and how destructive she can be to such a successful and well-respected male character:

> He had been pointed out as a very successful and well-known man about town. Hurstwood looked the part, for, besides being slightly under [40], he had a good, stout constitution, an active manner, and a solid, substantial air, which was composed in part of his fine clothes, his clean linen, his jewels, and above all, his own sense of importance. (45)

Before Hurstwood is introduced to Carrie, Dreiser provides an extensive elaboration on Hurstwood's past and present life, especially within his own household. His past is a story of success, gradually rising from bartender to manager. His present career is successful, but his family life is in shambles. He is gradually being alienated from his wife, Julia, his son, George Junior, and his daughter, Jessica. Ironically, Hurstwood's lack of understanding of his daughter's needs as a young woman is exactly what he will later be faced with in his relationship with Carrie:

> There was a time when he had been considerably enamored of his Jessica, especially when he was younger and more confined in his success. Now, however, in her [17th] year, Jessica had developed a certain amount of reserve and independence[,] which was not inviting to the richest form of parental devotion. She was in the high school, and had notions of life which were decidedly those of a patrician. She liked nice clothes and urged for them constantly. Thoughts of love and elegant individual establishments were running in her head. (83)

Hurstwood's problem is that he is fighting a battle between his outer successful life and his life at home. Outwardly, he appears to be the epitome of a successful businessman who has it all. Inwardly, he is discontented and is locked into a loveless marriage. His wife is shrewish, his children are spoiled, and he is getting older. Such a detailed background of Hurstwood may be intended on the part of Dreiser to show the helpless state of the deadly woman's victim.

When Drouet introduces Hurstwood to Carrie, she immediately senses the superiority of Hurstwood in intelligence, but more significantly, in the richness of his clothes: "When Hurstwood called, she met a man who was more clever than Drouet in a hundred ways. ... His clothes were particularly new and rich in appearance" (95). To Carrie, this is a more prosperous man who is a typical representative of the upper- middle class. Hurstwood dresses with more sophistication than Drouet, has better manners, and has more money. For these reasons, he has something more substantial to offer Carrie: "Carrie was thoroughly impressed "(98), until "it was driven into Carrie's mind that here was the superior man" (108). Although Lawrence E. Hussman, Jr., argues "Carrie's drift into her relationships with Drouet and Hurstwood is handled in such a way that conscious decisions do not seem to be involved" (22), Carrie does seem to be conscious and deliberate in her choice of men. She is calculating and shrewd in her choices.

According to Lehan, in the holograph and early scripts of the novel, Dreiser endows Carrie with a manipulative mind and portrays her as a woman who is willing to undertake daring actions. He later changes his plans and makes her appear more maidenly and less smart than she was in the manuscript to facilitate the process of getting the novel published. Upon close examination of the deleted passages, it is my opinion that it is clear that Carrie is far less innocent and more cunning than she appears to be. For example, in the description of one of Carrie's walks with Hurstwood, Dreiser deleted a passage in which Hurstwood pulls "a thin clean roll of new $100 bills out of his vest" and gives one to Carrie. In the holograph, she hesitates and then takes it: "Carrie could hardly refuse the offer he was so tactful about it. He put it in her little green leather purse and closed it up" (Lehan 60–61).

Hurstwood is blinded by his passion for Carrie, and therefore, we witness him committing one fatal flaw after another. Like McTeague, who is immediately captivated by Trina, from the moment Hurstwood meets Carrie, he is captivated by her majestic powers as a femme fatale: "He had been thinking almost uninterruptedly of her. Her leniency had, in a way, inflamed his regard. He felt that he must succeed with her, and that speedily" (119). The more Hurstwood is captivated, the better Carrie feels about herself and the more she realizes how much power she has: "Here was the greatest mystery, the man of money and affairs sitting beside her, appealing to her. Behold, he had ease and comfort, his strength was great, his position high, his clothing rich, and yet he was appealing to her" (125). And in the process of captivating Hurstwood, the physical features and the seductive beauty of the femme fatale emerge, features which have not been mentioned by Dreiser before. We now are made aware of the dark hair, the captivating eyes, the attractive figure, as well as the pallid complexion, the features that captivate her male victim, who "was charmed by the pale face, the lissome figure, draped in pearly gray, with a coiled string of pearls at the throat" (178). Because Dreiser does not describe her in the beginning of the novel as a femme fatale with the physical characteristics needed to be identified as one, Dreiser's intention is to show a femme fatale in the making. She does not come into the city as one, yet she is created by the atmosphere of the city and the men she encounters there. Because of what takes place in the city, these characteristics emerge and become visible, especially visible when she is in the process of charming Hurstwood, her primary victim.

The strength of Hurstwood's desire for Carrie becomes overwhelming and causes him to lose control of his reason and emotions. At the same time, Carrie grows more and more powerful, taking pleasure in "the atmosphere which this man created for her" (191). However, her dreams of happiness with Hurstwood are shattered when she realizes that Hurstwood is a married man. Instead of being angry at herself for allowing him in her life in the first place, she is angry at Drouet for introducing her to Hurstwood, and she is angry at Hurstwood for being married "not because she respects the rights of marriage but because Hurstwood has compromised his ability to support her" (Lehan 60). Drouet leaves Carrie after their argument, and in another scene, which Dreiser deleted from the holograph, we witness Carrie calculating and trying to figure a way out of her misfortune. Dreiser deleted the agony Carrie faces because of the fact that Drouet leaves, her fear of once again being alone and of "what would happen if she were again thus rudely thrown upon her resources" (Lehan 61).

Hurstwood's and Carrie's public appearances together anger Hurstwood's wife, and his wife ultimately files a scandalous divorce suit. The escalating anger of his wife coupled with the fear of losing his public image trigger Hurstwood to commit crime. Hurstwood robs Fitzgerald and Moy's safe in a scene that vividly asserts the weakness of the human will. Having committed the crime, Hurstwood starts calculating his losses, which include his family, property, position, reputation, and Carrie. He does not want to lose Carrie, but amazingly, he is willing to sacrifice everything else: "It is to be observed that the man did not justify himself to himself. He was not troubling about that. His whole thought was the possibility of persuading Carrie" (240). The fact that he is thinking only about Carrie shows the extent to which Carrie has power over him. He is blinded by his passion, unable to ponder his acts, mystified and intrigued by the power Carrie has over him. After stealing the money, an act caused by his infatuation with Carrie and his weakness as a human being, he is faced with the problem of convincing Carrie to go away with him. He has to lie to Carrie to get her to go away with him.

On the train, Carrie is seemingly angered by Hurstwood's course of action. However, she weakly struggles and easily succumbs, comforted by the thought that she has found herself a means of support by being with Hurstwood, and by the thought of the new and strange places to where he may take her, keeping in mind that Drouet has already abandoned her and she has no means of financial support: "It was an interesting world to her. Her life had just begun. She did not feel herself defeated at all" (260).

In New York, the femme fatale gradually takes full control of their lives. We witness Hurstwood's life taking a downward turn, while, on the other hand, Carrie's life takes an upward spin. They live together for three years, merely getting by with the interest that Hurstwood earns from a saloon. He loses his job there and spends the remainder of the money he has paying their living expenses and playing cards. Meanwhile, Carrie gets a job as a chorus girl and starts supporting the household. Hurstwood becomes desperate enough to take a job as a strike-breaker but quits in fear of his life. During this time, Carrie does not offer Hurstwood any kind of moral support or encouragement, and she only takes into consideration the money she is spending on the household and how much she would rather spend it solely on herself. She does not comprehend how hard Hurstwood is trying to adjust to his life in New York, how degraded he feels, and how much he is suffering, especially after trying to work at the railroad company: "Those who look upon Hurstwood's Brooklyn venture as an error of judgment will none the less realize the negative influence on him of the fact that he had tried and failed. Carrie got a wrong idea of it" (396).

Eventually, as Carrie grows more and more popular and makes more money, she abandons Hurstwood without any regret. Hurstwood takes a job doing scullery work in a hotel but comes down with pneumonia. He loses his job, becomes a beggar, and eventually commits suicide, thinking "what's the use?" of his whole life after Carrie had destroyed his past, present, and future (462).

Carrie carefully chooses the appropriate time to rid herself of Hurstwood. Carrie could have abandoned Hurstwood at an earlier time when he confessed to her that they were never legally married, but she did not do so because Hurstwood at that time was still supporting her. She abandons him when he becomes entirely dependent on her and only when she is able to sufficiently support herself. The career Dreiser chooses for Carrie is most appropriate for the femme fatale who has been created by the city. In Chicago, she longs to be an actress and performs in an amateur play. In New York, she begins as a chorus girl and makes her way up. Her entire life in both cities is based upon putting on an act. At first, she lives with Drouet and, at the same time, she dates Hurstwood, lying to Drouet when he asks her about how many times Hurstwood had been there to call on her. She lives with Hurstwood in New York, and when she finds a job for herself, she starts lying to him about how much money she is making and about how and with whom she spends her time. She promotes her career by making the audience laugh when the comedian asks her, "well, who are you?" and she replies, "I am yours truly" (396). This is what Carrie's life has been all about, pretending to be "yours truly" to the men she lives with, then abandoning them whenever she finds an opportunity to advance, especially financially, in her life. She is motivated by a strong desire for comfort and wealth, and she disregards the feelings of her male victims. Hurstwood's deterioration is partly his own fault; however, he is victimized by Carrie, who uses him as a means to improve her life. Once she realizes her mistake, she does not take into consideration the sacrifices that Hurstwood has made for her sake. She also fails to nourish and sustain the love and passion that he once had for her. The only thing that she cares for is her love of herself.

The idea of consumerism comes into play with regard to Carrie and her relationship to both Drouet and Hurstwood. Blanche H. Gelfant explains how integrated the idea of consumerism is in literary naturalism in general and in *Sister Carrie* in particular. Gelfant explains: "In *Sister Carrie*, the mediation of consumerism through a woman's desire produced a sequence of seeing, wanting, consuming, and being consumed..." (191). Gelfant, however, fails to acknowledge the fact that Carrie herself is not only to be seen as the consumed, but also as the consumer who has been able to consume not only commodities, but also the men that she lives with.

The Fall of the Femme Fatale
There is yet one more man who enters the life of Carrie. Drouet functions as the creator of the femme fatale, and Hurstwood functions as the victim of the femme fatale. Robert Ames is also introduced in the novel. Critics have usually viewed him as the spokesman of Drieser. Hussman asserts that Ames "appears to function as the author's spokesman in offering Carrie some perspective on her pursuits and in pointing the way to what he thinks may be her higher calling" (24). Lehan sees him as "the sincere advisor" who encourages Carrie to climb higher (65), an idea reiterated by McAleer who believes that Ames motivates Carrie to aim higher (83).

Ames is an intriguing character who appears in two extended scenes late in the novel. Carrie is introduced to Mr. Ames through her neighbor and friend, Mrs. Vance. During the course of one of their gourmet dinners in a fancy restaurant, "Carrie studied the company with open eyes. So this was high life in New York. It was so that the rich spent their days and evenings." Ames does not like this lifestyle and comments to Carrie, "Do you know... I sometimes think it is a shame for people to spend so much money this way" (299). Ames confuses Carrie with his remarks about this shallow lifestyle, and he also directs her attention to the fact that there is more to life than just money. This makes Carrie think:

> She felt as if she would like to be agreeable to this young man, and also there came with it, or perhaps preceded it,

the slightest shade of a feeling that he was better educated than she was—that his mind was better. He seemed to look it, and the saving grace in Carrie was that she could understand that people could be wiser. She had seen a number of people in her life who reminded her of what she had vaguely come to think of as scholars. This strong young man beside her, with his clear natural look, seemed to get a hold of things which she did not quite understand. (300)

As their conversation continues, Carrie compares Ames to both Drouet and Hurstwood, in the same way she compared Drouet to Hurstwood in her first encounter with Hurstwood: "He [Ames] seemed wiser than Hurstwood, saner and brighter than Drouet. He [Ames] seem[ed] innocent and clean, and she thought that he was exceedingly pleasant. She noticed, also, that his interest in her was a far-off one" (301). The scene culminates with Carrie returning to her apartment, where "she was rocking and beginning to see" (301). In this first encounter with Ames, Carrie, for the first time, is introduced to a man who is not interested in her physical beauty and her sexual appeal. Ames goes beyond all that is physical and introduces her to a higher level of thinking. Moreover, due to the fact that with the presence of a femme fatale, typically, there is a character that opposes her course of action, Ames can be seen as the opposing figure who does not agree with the course of action that the femme fatale is taking.

The second scene in which Carrie encounters Ames is at the very end of the novel when Carrie is at the peak of her success. This success, to Ames, is insignificant: "As a matter of fact, her little newspaper fame was nothing at all to him. He thought she could have done better, by far" (445). For the first time in the novel, Carrie is being advised to make better use of herself and her beauty. Ames exposes Carrie's follies, advises her to stop being selfish, explains to her the cycles of life, and asks her to

find a new path for herself instead of the femme fatale path she
has chosen:

> You have this quality in your eyes and mouth and in your
> nature. You can lose it, you know. If you turn away from
> it and live to satisfy yourself alone, it will go fast enough.
> The look will leave your eyes. Your mouth will change.
> Your power to act will disappear. You may think they
> won't, but they will. Nature takes care of that. (448)

And his parting words to her are "If I were you, …I'd change"
(446).

After her conversation with Ames, Carrie matures into a
woman who has a better understanding of life. Dreiser uses the
name Ames as an indicator of the fact that there is an aim to
her encounter with Ames. Carrie drifts from one man to another,
she achieves success, and she finally has all that money can buy
her. However, she does not feel that there is more to life until
her second encounter with Ames, who explains to her that life
is cyclical and the physical beauty she is enjoying and taking
advantage of now will one day fade. Ames' opposing point of
view elevates Carrie's understanding of life. For this reason,
Ames plays an important role in the novel, specifically in the life
of Carrie, although he appears only twice in the novel. Ames
kills the femme fatale spirit that has been kindled in Carrie by
life in the big city. McAleer emphasizes the fact that Ames' function in the novel is "to vindicate for her [Carrie] that she had
reached no true peak of accomplishment" (79), and David E.
Sloane emphasizes, "[H]is [Ames'] impact on Carrie is intellectual, for he is the agent for the development of a new and
enlarged circle of yearnings in her soul" (132).

Unfortunately, with this better understanding of life, Carrie
ends up as a dead-in-life character. Ames does kill the femme

fatale in spirit and does lead her to a higher level of thinking. However, Carrie is unhappy with her discoveries. The ending of the novel signifies the defeat of the femme fatale, who has been created by heredity, environment, the city, Drouet, and Hurstwood. Yet for Carrie to come to the realization that she has been defeated and has not achieved true success, Dreiser brings in Ames, who advises her to act in dramatic plays rather than comedies, signifying the importance of taking her life more seriously and thinking about the consequences of her actions as a femme fatale. In the end of the novel, Carrie is different. She thinks about her past actions: "Amid the tinsel and shine of her state walked Carrie, unhappy. As when Drouet took her, she had thought: 'Now I am lifted into that which is best'; as when Hurstwood seemingly offered her the better way: 'Now am I happy'" (464). She thinks about her futile present:

> And now Carrie had attained that which in the beginning seemed life's object, or, at least, such fraction of it as human beings ever attain of their original desires. She could look about on her gowns and carriage her furniture, and bank account. Friends there were...Applause there was, and publicity—once far off, essential things, but now grown trivial and insignificant. Beauty also—her type of loveliness—and yet she was lonely. (462)

And she contemplates her obscure future: "[S]he had learned that in this world, as in her own present state, was not happiness" (464).

The order in which Drouet, Hurstwood, and Ames are introduced into Carrie's life follows the linear order in which the femme fatale is created, blossoms, and then dies. Drouet, the seducer, introduces Carrie to her capabilities as a woman. Hurstwood is the victim of the femme fatale. With Hurstwood, Carrie slowly takes command of their life together, and simultaneously, she rises in the world, thus bringing Hurstwood to his ultimate ruin. Ames is the voice of reason who explains to Carrie that this path she is following will, under no circumstances, be eternal, and hence causes the death of the femme fatale and the birth of the lonely, melancholic, new Carrie.

Each of the three men has a different role to play in the life of the femme fatale, and, therefore, Dreiser creates each man differently. Drouet, the seducer, is able to maintain throughout the novel a balance between his head and his heart. He gives in to temptation but does not allow his instincts to govern his life. When he finds out about Carrie's relationship with Hurstwood, he simply leaves Carrie, a step he would have taken eventually but one triggered by his discovery of the relationship. He never does intend to marry Carrie, and to him, she is merely one of the women with whom he entertains himself. In the end of the novel, he is the same Drouet we meet in the beginning of the novel: "A good dinner, the company of a young woman, and an evening at the theater were the chief things for him" (458). He is unchanged, still working as a salesman, still prosperous, and still in pursuit of pretty women. Hurstwood, on the other hand, is never able to maintain a balance between his head and his heart after his encounter with Carrie. The once successful businessman becomes impulsive, careless, and thoughtless. Hussman asserts, "[T]he strength of Hurtswood's desire for Carrie is overwhelming—his passion is no longer colored with reason" (22). Like McTeague, animalistic instincts and his sexual need for Carrie rule his decisions, blind him, and lead to his tragic end.

Ames is the voice of reason in the novel. He is the only male character who is not interested in Carrie's physical attractiveness and is ruled by his mind and intellectual power. Because of his intellectuality, he is able to influence and bring about a change in Carrie, a change that would not have taken place without his interference and guidance. His work in an electrical company is metaphorical and serves as a means of providing light for people who are misguided, such as Carrie.

Not only do the three men in Carrie's life contribute to the rise and fall of the femme fatale, but also the women Carrie encounters in the big city play a significant part in her life as a femme fatale. Her sister, Minnie, provides Carrie with an example of a woman she would not aspire to be like. Caught in a loveless marriage, Minnie is "now a thin, though rugged, woman of twenty-seven, with ideas of life colored by her husband's, and fast hardening into narrower conceptions of pleasure and duty than had ever been hers in a thoroughly circumscribed youth" (19). Minnie stands in sharp contrast with Carrie: "Carrie, on the other hand, had the blood of youth and some imagination" (52). Carrie's stay at her sister's household is a brief one. Carrie wants to have a good time and entertain herself while she is in the big city. She also wants to enjoy spending the money she is making at the shoe factory, despite the fact that it is an insignificant amount of money. Therefore, Carrie breaks with her family and escapes with Droeut.

In New York, Carrie associates with and befriends her neighbor, Mrs. Vance. Carrie is well aware of the contrasts between herself and Mrs. Vance as their relationship develops. First of all, Mrs. Vance is legally married to her husband, unlike Carrie, who is Hurstwood's mistress. Second, Mrs. Vance and her husband are wealthy. Third, Mrs. Vance and her husband enjoy and entertain themselves with the abundance of money they possess. Mrs. Vance plays the piano and can afford to dress herself elegantly and extravagantly, a factor that particularly disturbs Carrie to a great extent. When, for example, Carrie sees Mrs. Vance elegantly wearing a dark blue dress, "this woman pained her by contrast." Moreover, Mrs. Vance "seemed to have so many dainty little things which Carrie had not. There were trinkets of gold, an elegant green leather purse set with her initials, a fancy handkerchief, exceedingly rich in design, and the like" (288). Carrie, who has never been able to rid herself of the strong grip of commodities, is envious of this woman and aspires to be like her. Mrs. Vance plays a significant role in making Carrie contemplate breaking free from Hurstwood and the poverty-stricken lifestyle she is living while with Hurstwood. Carrie

> could not, for the life of her, assume the attitude and smartness of Mrs. Vance, who, in her beauty, was all assurance...It cut her to the quick, and she resolved that she would not come here [Broadway] again until she looked better. At the same time she longed to feel the delight of parading here as an equal. Ah, then she would be happy! (289)

In *Godey's Lady's Book*, a popular magazine at the time, an entire section of the magazine entitled "Doings in New York" explains how people like Mrs. Vance come into society and bring about envy to the less fortunate, like Carrie for instance:

> The people who really enjoy society are those...fortunate newcomers, who, by judicious expenditure of money, flattery, good dinners, and other aids to social success have managed to attain the object of their ambition and see their names in the list with social stars of acknowledged magnitude. (295)

Because of the wide social gap between Mrs. Vance and Carrie, Carrie chooses to leave, and the more time Carrie spends with Mrs. Vance, the more determined she becomes to abandon Hurstwood and find a better opportunity for herself. Moreover, the same magazine explains how amateur theatricals became very popular at that time, and how fate has been favorable to Carrie, who has always been looking for a window of opportunity to better herself: "There is a craze in New York just now for amateur theatricals...A very small percentage of those who are fired by this ambition, ever appear on the real stage" (293). The fact that Carrie has been fortunate enough to appear on stage is a factor that Dreiser takes into consideration as the femme fatale eventually takes full control of her life and of Hurstwood.

The third woman in Carrie's life is her colleague in the theater, Lola Osborne. Lola's part in Carrie's life is to guide her in the work field and to aid her in bettering her opportunities. Unaware of the presence of Hurstwood in Carrie's life, Lola also talks Carrie into moving in with her and sharing the rent, an arrangement gladly accepted by Carrie. Moreover, Lola introduces Carrie to the carefree lifestyle of single women who can be festive and happy without any household obligations.

Having been exposed to her sister's lifestyle in Chicago, Mrs. Vance's lifestyle in New York, and Lola's lifestyle on Broadway, Carrie is motivated to break free and abandon Hurtswood. She does not want to stay with this man and end up like her sister. Moreover, Carrie now sees that the state to which Hurstwood has declined is similar to the state of Mr. Hanson, Minnie's husband. Hurstwood has grown accustomed to sitting by the radiator in their dreary flat, reading his newspaper, aloof from life, and dead in spirit. Pizer explains the scene where Carrie comes back home one night and thus finds Hurstwood:

> Carrie returns to her drab New York flat and finds Hurstwood sitting by the radiator reading his newspaper. The sight throws her into a mood of despair, a mood which has its origin—unknown to her and unexplained by Dreiser—in her subconscious recollection of the dour Hanson reading his newspaper each evening while waiting for his supper. If Hurstwood is Hanson, Carrie is becoming Minnie—a role

> which had repelled her from her earliest Chicago days. It
> is the emotional weight upon Carrie's subconscious of a
> series of such discrete "physical" moments in her relation-
> ship with Hurstwood in New York which compels her to
> leave him, though she consciously attributes her motive to
> a need for new clothes. (*The Novels of Theodore* 86)

Furthermore, Carrie has been introduced to the high style of living through Mrs. Vance, and she has also been introduced to
the carefree lifestyle of young and single women. The femme
fatale is in full force when she deserts Hurstwood and eventually abandons him without any sympathy or regret, thinking that
she will find her happiness by living like Mrs. Vance and Lola.

Trina and Carrie
Having taken a close look at Carrie's transformation from an
innocent young woman into a threatening femme fatale, and having examined her relationship with the men and women that she
encounters in the city, it might be useful to compare Carrie to
Trina. Both novels were written within the same time frame, and
Norris was one of the few admirers of the works of Theodore Dreiser, specifically *Sister Carrie*. Having been created by two different novelists at the turn of the twentieth century, the two female
protagonists as femmes fatales have very much in common.

First and foremost, both women are dangerous and deadly.
Trina needs to escape from her background and so does Carrie.
Trina's physical attractiveness appeals to Marcus and McTeague
the way Carrie's physical attractiveness appeals to Drouet and
Hurstwood. Trina marries McTeague to satisfy her animalistic
instincts, to escape from her family, and to secure herself in a
good marriage. Similarly, Carrie gives in to Drouet to escape
from her sister's household and to secure herself financially.
She further supposedly marries Hurstwood to escape from going
back to the streets after Drouet abandons her. Furthermore, both

women are obsessed with money; Trina likes to save it whereas
Carrie enjoys spending it. Both women do not have children—
another important aspect with regard to the femmes fatales.
Trina's inability to conceive may be explained in terms of her
animalistic mating with McTeague. Carrie's inability to conceive
may be explained in terms of the novelist's dissociation of Carrie from the traditional consequences of a sexual fall—disgrace,
pregnancy, and perhaps death. Pizer argues, "Although Carrie is a
'fallen woman,' she suffers few of the pangs and none of the mis-
fortunes of the type" (*The Novels of Theodore* 38). Both women
control their male counterparts until the men are forced to leave.
Trina ends up brutally murdered by McTeague, and McTeague
ends up in Death Valley handcuffed to the dead body of Marcus, walking in the desert without water, and will eventually face
his death. Carrie ends up lonely, discontented, and miserable—a
dead-in-life character despite her success on the stage—whereas
Hurstwood commits suicide, thinking to himself, "Wasn't good
enough for you [Carrie], was I? Huh!" (465).

Although both women have much in common given the fact
that both are femmes fatales, there are some differences between
the two women that need to be mentioned. Trina is born and
raised in the city, a place typically associated with experience.
Therefore, she is born a femme fatale and created as one. In order
to escape her hereditary traits, she is motivated by psychological
reasons to use her sexuality to control men. Carrie, on the other
hand, is born and raised in the countryside, a place typically associated with innocence. She does not set out to the big city with the
intention of being a femme fatale. However, in order to escape
her immediate cruel environment, she comes to the realization
that she has to use her sexuality in order to survive in this com-
petitive place. Therefore, Carrie is molded into a femme fatale.
She is motivated by social factors rather than psychological ones.

Both women choose to use their sexuality, asserting their free will, but are, nevertheless, eventually defeated.

In her book, *Women, Compulsion, Modernity: The Moment of American Naturalism*, Jennifer L. Fleissner argues that both McTeague and Hurstwood are "impotent males," and she provides an extensive comparison between Trina and Carrie. In both novels, Fleissner suggests, there are scenes which show older men, out of a job, begging for money from their female counterparts. These women, who are cold, rational, and pitiless, respond with a selfish regard for their own savings. Thus, the male hero is transformed into a version of the victimized "fallen woman." Fleissner adds,

> The fact that the women's monetary power gets persistently linked to the mysterious workings of luck or chance—Trina wins the lottery, ...Carrie's success depends on random lucky breaks throughout—merely underscores this construal of the men as, in highly traditional terms, victims of a heartless fate. (20)

Fleissner concludes by asserting that novels such as *McTeague* and *Sister Carrie* belong to the turn-of-the-century literature in which modern wives rule "by hysteria and melancholy" and become the "victimizer of choice of the period's self-pityingly marginalized male," wresting "the reins of economic selfhood" from his grasp. Looked at from this perspective, Fleissner validates the idea that American naturalism has created femmes fatales, women acting "as part of the array of pitiless natural forces threatening men" (20–21). Women such as Trina and Carrie are themselves victims of a naturalistic world, but they do take action against the naturalistic world by using their femininity and the power that comes along with it and become destructive forces to the men that fall under their spell.

There is little agreement among critics about what sort of woman Carrie represents. Carrie has been regarded as a character who is weak, unintelligent, and powerless—a character fully controlled by the environment created by the big city. The might of the big city not only captivates her but also controls her, hence her fall. Seen from this perspective, Carrie is a controlled character whose fall is not her responsibility. She is "a victim of external events, and particularly in her responses to men she appears to be dominated by conditions over which she had little control" (Riggio 26). Sloane sympathizes with Carrie and calls her "a tragic heroine" with "mediocre nonintellectual capacity" (85). To these critics, Caroline Meeber is the downtrodden, naturalistic female character, the victim of fate who rises in the world as a reward for her patience and endurance.

Some critics, on the other hand, see Carrie as "calloused" and driven by "hard cold selfishness," "a narcissistic young woman in whom self-interest runs high." Carrie is also a "quick learner" possessed of a "sharp eye," whose aim is to "climb a ladder" through her relationships with men (Gerber 56). Caroline Drouet and Caroline Wheeler are the two other names she has that validate the claim that she is interested only in herself and uses the names of the men she is living with as a vehicle to step higher in life.

Yet, critics have not seen Carrie as a femme fatale, although Lundquist argues, "if [Carrie] is not quite a femme fatale, she is far more than the ordinary…woman" (33). Nevertheless, the evidence for the presence of the femme fatale is clear. Caroline Meeber goes to the city innocent and naïve, unaware of what she can achieve with her charm and beauty. Upon encountering Drouet, Carrie understands that in order to avoid the humiliating kind of life she experienced in the shoe factory, she must make use of her sexuality, hence she adopts the name Caroline Drouet. Upon encountering Hurstwood, Carrie is at the peak of her beauty and instantly captivates him. She emerges as a femme fatale with dark hair, a pale face, an attractive figure, and enchanting eyes. Similar to Trina's effect on McTeague, Carrie has Hurstwood under a spell and brings out the animalistic instincts in the successful businessman. Hurstwood's life moves from bad to worse as Hurstwood loses his capacity to think clearly and reasonably after his encounter with Carrie, hence his suicide. Carrie is neither a tragic heroine nor a victim. She is the victimizer who seeks to take control instead of being controlled—this is Carrie Madenda. Her behavior is neither self-negating nor self-abnegating; it is self-defining. She seeks to define herself by using the power she has as a woman. Her various uses of the names she chooses for herself indicate how quickly she adapts to her surroundings and becomes in command of the relationships with the men she lives with. She is guided in her choices by self-protective instincts and is aided by her charming power as a femme fatale. She rises in the world as a result of her free will, but alas, despite her triumph on the stage, she will still fight battles of loneliness, sadness, and isolation in an evil, naturalistic world, battles which will not be overcome by the femme fatale. The lamentable wail with which Dreiser concludes the novel voices Carrie's longings and fears:

> Oh Carrie, Carrie! Oh, blind strivings of the human heart!…Know, then, that for you is neither surfeit nor content. In your rocking chair, by your window dreaming, shall you long alone. In your rocking chair, by your window, shall you dream such happiness as you may never feel. (465)

Carrie is an innocent young woman who comes to the big city to find employment and happiness. Yet, she finds herself facing a merciless, industrial, materialistic world, and thus, her dreams of happiness are shattered. She understands that, in order to survive, she has to give up all the moral values upon which she has been raised. Thus, instead of becoming the victim of the city, she shrewdly becomes the victimizer of men. She gradually rises in the big city because of her will to succeed, but despite her rise, she finds herself alone and in a mood of despair. This is the price that Carrie pays for her victimization. Carrie's acts are not moral in any way, yet it would be difficult to say that they are immoral after witnessing how harsh the city can be. In fact, the common man, or rather woman in the case of Carrie, is fighting battles of existence, where the law of survival of the fittest is applied everywhere in society. She struggles to find a place for herself in the world; she does so at the expense of Drouet and Hurstwood and lives by a code of selfish amoralism. Pizer explains the amorality of the characters in the novel, especially Carrie's amorality and asserts in creating Carrie's character that:

> Dreiser sought to depict less a character's confusion about life than the very confusion at the center of life itself— the seeming haphazard but subterraneanly directed currents of experience, the amoral need most individuals have to fulfill themselves in a world controlled by moral assumptions, and the pathetically superficial but moving instances of man's pursuit of beauty. (*The Novels of Theodore* 72)

Carrie lives solely for herself; unfortunately, Carrie will live by herself in spiritual emptiness and will never find true happiness. The story of Carrie is the story of an insignificant woman, caught in an unkind, cruel, industrial world that has compelled her to use her femininity and charm. Carrie becomes successful and realizes how rich she is now; unfortunately, she also realizes how poor she is and she acknowledges the emptiness of the state she has reached. She discovers that the golden treasures she has been seeking to attain are illusory.

CHAPTER 4

"A LANGUAGE WHICH NOBODY UNDERSTOOD:" EDNA PONTELLIER AS FEMME FATALE IN KATE CHOPIN'S *THE AWAKENING*

Kate Chopin's turn-of-the-nineteenth-century novel *The Awakening* portrays Edna Pontellier as a representative, middle-class American woman who is searching for meaning in life. Her childhood life is complex, and this complexity intensifies as she gets older and marries to Mr. Pontellier. This chapter places *The*

Awakening in a social, historical context and explains how Edna emerges as a femme fatale, given the fact that she was created by a female author. The chapter closely examines Edna's past background and environment as well as her present, immediate surroundings, and explains why Edna chooses the femme fatale path. This chapter not only highlights Edna's relationship to the men in her life (Mr. Pontellier, Robert Lebrun, and Alcee Arobin), but it also highlights Edna's relationship to the women in her life (Madame Ratignolle and Mademoiselle Reisz). Throughout the chapter, Edna will be compared to the female protagonists discussed in the previous two chapters, placing particular emphasis on the gender of the writer who is responsible for creating each femme fatale. The chapter concludes with an interpretation of Edna's suicide.

Before taking a closer look at Edna's background and environment, it might be useful to provide an account of the background against which the novel was written. Written at the end of the nineteenth century, the novel depicts the tension between the old and the new, the traditional and the modern. Changes were taking place in the roles of women and how they were perceived in society. The traditional, fixed role of women was that of domesticity and obedience, hence marital bliss. Kate Chopin, as well as other women, were concerned with the ascribed role of women and were beginning to plant the roots of modern feminism during the 1890s (Dyer 6).

Margaret Culley provides a background that assists in the understanding of the social context of the novel. Being labeled as a decade of change and social tension, the 1890s was a period when several major events took place that influenced the transformation of American society. Culley explains, "[T]he depression of the 1890s accentuated class division, and urbanization and industrialization continued to challenge traditional ways of life" (119). According to Culley, changing social norms at the turn of the twentieth century were associated with the changing roles of women in society. In one sense, rapid industrial growth opened more low-wage working opportunities to lower class white women, such as the job we find Carrie taking on in the beginning of *Sister Carrie*. Middle-class white women, on the other hand, had begun to gain opportunities to attend college and to enter professions that previously were restricted to men (119). Culley points out that the increased opportunities in the job market in the late nineteenth century altered the structure of society: "By removing production from the home, [industrialization] had provided these new wage-earning jobs for women" (4). Women's servitude to the domestic realm was altered as educational and working opportunities expanded. This background information helps to explain the social influences that create Edna as a femme fatale. Culley emphasizes that women's attempts to improve their social condition paralleled social development in the period. Edna's ambition to become independent represents a changing woman's role. In addition to wanting to be economically independent, Edna transgresses and wants to liberate herself sexually. By defying social limitations, Edna is making way for her sexual awakening as well. Society, however, was not prepared for the radical changes that Edna was advocating.

In 1898, one year before the publication of *The Awakening*, Charlotte Perkins Gilman published *Women and Economics*. The book advocates women becoming more economically independent, thereby improving their marriages and fulfilling themselves by being productive members within the household. Gilman felt, as Chopin did, that relationships founded on economic dependence and expectations about the performance of household duties needed to be reexamined. Gilman wrote, "Marriage is not perfect unless it is between class equals. There is no equality in class between those who do their share in the world's work in the largest, newest, highest ways, and those who do theirs in the smallest, oldest, lowest ways" (220). Gilman argues that a person's class is determined by their social and economic environment, an argument already well established in American naturalism, but Gilman stresses the fact that the human female's social and economic dependence is unnatural and artificial—that of economic dependence on the male:

> We are the only animal species in which the female depends upon the male for food, the only animal species in which sex-relation is also an economic relation. With us an entire sex lives in a relation of economic dependence upon the other sex. (5)

Gilman concludes that women's energy is locked up and wrongfully-oriented toward making themselves pleasing to men due to the fact of their economic dependency. Gilman urges a variety of changes that will alter women's condition of economic dependence, the most important of which is "to break up that relic of the patriarchal age—the family as an economic unit" (151). In *The Awakening*, Chopin seems to be responding to Gilman's ideas, and she questions the traditional role of women and presents the character of Edna, a woman who is willing to undertake the challenge against the dominant patriarchal world.

Larzer Ziff points out in *The American 1890s: Life and Times of a Lost Generation* that there were other writers in the 1890s besides Chopin who questioned the traditional role of women. Larzer argues, "to be a serious female author in the [90s] was to be a writer of stories about women and their demands" (283). Authors like Ellen Glasgow and Theodore Dreiser were looking at the effects of urban living on relationships between men and women. Chopin, however, not only examines the effects of urban living on the relationship between men and women but also, through a character like Edna Pontellier, is transgressing sexually and exploring female passion, which at that time was thought to be immoral and unhealthy. With works such as *McTeague* and *Sister Carrie*, emphasis is placed on the effects of industrialism and materialism on the male character through the victimization of the female protagonist, who is also under the same effects. In addition to that, we witness the downfall of the male characters because of their uncontrollable passion and sexual needs when they encounter the femme fatale, hence their ruin. Caroline Meeber, for example, is seldom represented as a woman with sexual passion and sexual needs but is depicted as a woman who uses her sexual power to rise in the world. Chopin, however, speaks out strongly and aggressively about female eroticism through her character Edna. Edna is a woman who is asking for her place in the universe as an autonomous individual and is, at the same time, realizing and awakening to her feminine power, which will, ultimately, destroy her.

THE IMPRISONMENT OF EDNA

The novel opens with "a green and yellow parrot" trapped in "a cage outside the door," which keeps "repeating over and over… That's all right!" This parrot "could speak a little Spanish, and also a language which nobody understood" (43). The parrot is a caged animal who imitates the sounds it hears. This is the role Edna is supposed to take in the Creole society in which she finds herself entrapped. Chopin purposely uses the parrot—a bird known for its dullness, stupidity, and imitation. Yet, the parrot, besides being able to speak French and Spanish, speaks a language unintelligible to any except "the mocking-bird that hung on the other side of the door." The parrot's languages show how Edna can be an imitator and yet can discover a new form of verbal and possibly behavioral patterns that no one will be able to comprehend. The opening lines of the novel suggest that Edna will choose a different path, a path that has not been trod by any of the Creole women before—the path of the seductive, mysterious femme fatale.

Edna's childhood memories revolve around her search for freedom to express herself and searching for "a language which nobody understood." As a child, Edna constantly formed the habit of walking through the meadow to escape the tyranny of her gloomy father. Edna lost her mother at an early age, and instead of being brought up in a loving, tender environment that would make up for the loss of her mother, Edna found herself surrounded by harsh circumstances that eventually lead her to become self-contained: "[Edna] was not accustomed to an outward and spoken expression of affection either in herself or in others" (61).

During the summer at Grand Isle, Edna begins to analyze her past, the history of her self-constitution, and she perceives the basis for her self-alienation and reserve in her childhood's shortcomings. She grew up without a mother and with a very cold, unloving father. By analyzing her past, Edna is also taking a close look at her present situation. Upon being asked by Madame Ratignolle what she is thinking while both of them are relaxing near the sea, Edna replies,

> The hot wind beating in my face made me think—without any connection that I can trace—of a summer day in Kentucky, of a meadow that seemed as big as the ocean to the very little girl walking through the grass, which was higher than her waist. She threw out her arms as if swimming when she walked, beating the tall grass as one strikes out in the water. (60)

Yet, she unconsciously does connect her past to her present and sets forth a warning: "Sometimes I feel this summer as if I were walking through the meadow again; idly, aimlessly, unthinking, and unguided" (61).

Edna realizes at that moment that her present situation is lacking and that she has been striving to achieve her personal freedom and self-consciousness all her life. Edna finds herself confined within the boundaries of marriage. After having several childhood infatuations and fantasies about men, "her marriage to Leonce Pontellier was purely an accident, in this respect resembling many other marriages which masquerade as the decrees of Fate" (62). Revolting against her father and trying to escape from an unhappy childhood, Edna thinks that her marriage to Mr. Pontellier will make up for the attention and love she has been longing for:

> [Leonce Pontellier] pleased her; his absolute devotion flattered her. She fancied there was a sympathy of thought and taste between them, in which fancy she was mistaken. Add to this the violent opposition of her father and her sister Margaret to her marriage with a Catholic, and we need seek no further for the motives which led to accept Monsieur Pontellier for her husband. (62)

Edna realizes, however, that she has been mistaken in her choice. Instead of finding happiness and fulfillment within the institution of marriage, she finds herself more confined and more threatened. Instead of treating Edna as a human being, Mr. Pontellier "looks at his wife as one looks at a valuable piece of property" (44). The ring that symbolizes her marriage serves as a constant reminder to Edna of her entrapment within the marriage. The wedding ring appears in several scenes in the novel, all of which depict Edna struggling to rid herself of the ring and the obligations that come along with it, yet she always eventually puts it back on, suggesting the failure to step out of the boundaries of a locked, loveless marriage.

Like Carrie, who does not intend to use her sexuality as a means of escape from her surrounding circumstances until she finds out that her sexuality is in fact her only means of escape, Edna is faced with a somewhat similar situation. Edna finds herself falling in one trap after the other. She escapes from her father's household only to find herself in another prison created by the male patriarchy. Moreover, by marrying into Creole society, Edna is constantly looked at as an outsider who does not understand their way of life. Creole society dictates that its women find all their satisfactions through wifehood and motherhood. That same society produces ideal mother-women such as Adele Ratignolle but forbids women to develop any other talents or interests. After she escapes from an imprisoning past, Edna's present is even more confining: the domestic sphere, the social order, the family lifestyle of the Creoles do not suit Edna. As a result, Edna finds that her social life and personal development are circumscribed by socioeconomic forces as powerful as those that control the life of Carrie. She discovers that her life must be lived within socioeconomic and biological boundaries that are as unyielding as the big city that Carrie finds herself entrapped in. Edna wishes to find a way out of tradition and, therefore, chooses to speak, like the brightly colored parrot introduced on the novel's first page, "a language which nobody understood," except perhaps by other femme fatale figures like Trina and Carrie, who understand that there is power that can perhaps provide them, at least temporarily, with control over both heredity and the surrounding environment—the power of the feminine. Edna emerges as a femme fatale:

> Mrs. Pontellier's eyes were quick and bright; they were a yellowish brown, about the color of her hair. She had a way of turning them swiftly upon an object and holding them there as if lost in some inward maze of contemplation or thought.

Her eyebrows were a shade darker than her hair. They were
thick and almost horizontal, emphasizing the depth of her
eyes. She was rather handsome than beautiful. Her face
was captivating by reason of a certain frankness of expression and a contradictory subtle play of features. Her manner was engaging. (45–46)

Although Edna is similar to both Trina and Carrie in that she
takes advantage of her sexual power as a woman, Edna is different in that she is already a married woman. Both Trina and
Carrie are husband hunters who seek marriage as a means of
escape from harsher circumstances and as a means of secur-
ing themselves financially. Both end up in love with money
more than with the husbands they choose for themselves. However, with Edna, and given the fact that the creator of Edna is a
female writer, it is her husband as well as her economic dependency on her husband from which she needs to escape. Although
Edna "liked money as well as most women, and accepted it
with no little satisfaction," Edna, because of her creation by
a female writer, does not like the fact that her husband is the
sole provider of money; and despite the fact that "all the ladies
declared that Mr. Pontellier was the best husband in the world,"
Edna does not seem to agree with that (50). Edna's marriage is
defective because she does not feel she is a productive member
within the household and within society at large, a factor that
leads Mr. Pontellier to assume that Edna is a valuable possession rather than a recognized individual.

Like the state Hurstwood is in before he encounters Carrie,
Mr. Pontellier is a successful, middle-aged man whose main
concern is his business transactions and who, as a result of being
immersed in business, regards Edna as a "piece of property"
instead of as an individual human being. And although it may
appear that Mr. Pontellier is an insensitive husband, Mr. Pontellier

is merely acting in accordance with the Creole's way of life. He is immersed in a culture that idolizes the dedicated wife and "mother-woman." He cannot visualize any other option for women, and despite his possessiveness of Edna, Mr. Pontellier is depicted as a kind and generous man who cares for his wife and children. His lack of understanding of Edna's need for private space and her need to have "a position in the universe as a human being" apart from her place as a wife and a mother, however, leads to a wide gap in their marriage that will widen as Edna chooses to give way to her sexuality (57).

Edna's awakening to her sexuality is, therefore, created by her imprisonment. Constrained by religion, domesticity, family, property, and the patriarchal social order, Edna is a typical naturalistic character who finds herself, like the parrot, in a locked cage. Yet, Edna is a woman with a strong will and seeks to create her own way after she realizes that she has been constantly living in a fierce naturalistic as well as a paternal world. In both the cases of Trina and Carrie, the reader senses more of the power of the naturalistic world rather than the power of the paternal world because of the fact that both works were created by male authors. In *The Awakening*, however, Chopin purposely emphasizes the status of women who find themselves restricted by biological determinism within the patriarchal system. Edna realizes that she no longer desires to fulfill the expectations of other people, namely, the men who have authority over her (her father and her husband), and she sees her role as wife and mother as constrictive. She questions the dual life she is living: "that outward existence which conforms and the inward life which questions" (57), until she starts to find answers to her question:

> A certain light was beginning to dawn dimly within her—the light which showing the way, forbids it...

Mrs. Pontellier was beginning to realize her position in the universe as a human being, and to recognize her relations as an individual to the world within and about her. (57)

Edna Breaks Free

Having understood that she does, in fact, have a place in the universe, Edna frees herself of all of the constraints that have been obstructing her growth as a human being and as a woman in particular. She allows herself to experience the power of the feminine. Unlike Dreiser's Carrie, who needs a male character like Drouet to seduce and thus introduce her to her feminine power, Chopin's Edna does not need the help of a male character to do so. She discovers her power from within herself. The night in which she discovers her powers serves as a turning point in the novel, and it is the night which gives birth to the newly aroused sexual woman:

> A feeling of exultation overtook her, as of some power of significant import had been given her to control the working of her body and soul. She grew daring and reckless, overestimating her strength. She wanted to swim far out, where no woman had swum before...As she swam she seemed to be reaching out for the unlimited in which to lose herself. (73)

Incidentally, Robert Lebrun is with Edna when she awakens to her power as a woman. Up until that night, the night of August 29th, Edna has been casually spending time with Robert. However, when Edna awakens to her sexuality, Robert is with her and explains to her that a spirit has been haunting the seashore searching for "some one mortal worthy to hold him company, worthy of being exalted for a few hours into the realms of the semi-celestials," adding that the spirit's "search has always been hitherto fruitless, and he has sunk back, disheartened, into the sea" until "tonight he found Mrs. Pontellier. Perhaps he will never wholly release her from the spell" (75).

Not only does Edna fall under a spell, but she herself starts creating spells of her own. Edna becomes increasingly aware of her erotic impulses, and the first spell she chooses to cast is upon Robert Lebrun. Each summer, Robert chooses a married woman to innocently flirt with and entertain. This year he chooses Edna. At one point earlier, realizing that the situation could go beyond acceptable boundaries, Madame Ratignolle warns Robert of the effects Edna may have on him and strongly urges him to stay away from her, emphasizing that Edna is an outsider and is a woman who is distinctly different from the other Creole women: "She is not one of us; she is not like us. She might make the unfortunate blunder of taking you seriously" (64). However, Robert does not take Madame Ratignolle's advice until that very night when he witnesses Edna's transformation into an erotic, impulsive woman. From that point, Robert becomes cautious in his relationship with Edna. Unlike McTeague and Hurstwood who desperately fall in love with the femmes fatales they encounter, Robert is more aware of the consequences and effects of becoming involved with a femme fatale. He understands the imminent threat that Edna will have on him and leaves. Although Nancy Walker describes Robert as "a man who is too much of a gentleman to dally with a married woman" (16), I believe that Robert is not merely acting as a gentleman, but he is dealing with this woman with extreme caution, fearful of the spell that she can cast over him. This caution becomes evident in the way he behaves when he is around Edna. He is too attracted to her to be able to stay away, and at the same time, he is too afraid and hesitant to become too close to her. The advance/retreat strategy he uses indicates his ambivalence toward Edna and his fear of getting involved with her:

> The Pontelliers and Ratignolles walked ahead; the women leaning upon the arms of their husbands. Edna could hear Robert's voice behind them, and could sometimes hear what he said. She wondered why he did not join them. It was unlike him not to. Of late he had sometimes held away from her for an entire day, redoubling his devotion upon the next and the next, as though to make up for the hours that had been lost. (72)

A few days after Edna awakens to her sexual powers, Robert unexpectedly decides to leave and go to Mexico. His decision, however, should not be read as a sign of weakness, but rather as a sign of strength. Robert does not allow the femme fatale to take control over him and cast her spell upon him. His only option is to flee. Wendy Martin explains Edna's love for Robert by stating, "Her love for Robert consists of agonized longing and unrequited sexual need and seems to be a masochistic exercise in negative capability" (23). This may be true if the reader is to assume that Edna is exercising negative capability. However, given the fact that Edna has been transformed into a femme fatale and looked at from the perspective of Robert, her love for him can be read as a sadistic exercise not in negative capability, but rather in positive capability in asserting herself by exploring her power as a woman and, more important, as a femme fatale. By entrapping Robert, she is not negating herself, and Robert, who is not weak but shrewd, understands the consequences of getting involved with such a woman. Robert's final choice is to retreat.

After Robert leaves, Edna feels that his going "had some way taken the brightness, the color, the meaning out of everything. The conditions of her life were in no way changed, but her whole existence was dulled, like a faded garment which seems to be no longer worth wearing" (95). During his absence, Edna realizes that she has not been able to victimize Robert, and her passion for him increases. Edna needs to exercise the power she has awakened to, but Robert does not allow her to do so with him. Therefore, she turns her attention to Alcee Arobin.

Alcee Arobin is another flirtatious bachelor who "admired Edna extravagantly" (128). Like Drouet, Arobin is a realistic, practical character who takes each day as it comes and does not allow the femme fatale to take control of him. He talks sweetly and gently to Edna and rekindles the desires she has had for Robert but has not been able to fulfill. He acts as a substitute for Robert, and although her feelings for Arobin are not as strong as her feelings toward Robert, Edna, nevertheless, "wanted something to happen—something, anything; she did not know what" (129). Edna admits to herself, "Alcee Arobin was absolutely nothing to her. Yet, his presence, his manners, the warmth of his glances, and above all the touch of his lips upon her hand had acted like a narcotic upon her" and help her, once again, to realize her strength as a woman (132). The same scene is echoed in *Sister Carrie*, when Drouet caresses the hands of Carrie in the process of seducing her, and at the same time, brings her to a better understanding of her sexual powers. Like Drouet, who assists Carrie in providing her with all the material things that her heart desires, Arobin's presence in Edna's life helps her fulfill her desires, not material, but rather emotional and sexual desires of fulfilling herself. As far as he is concerned, he will not let Edna cast a spell over him and will please himself with her as long as possible. At one point Edna warns him: "I am a devilishly wicked specimen of the sex," but he does not take her warnings seriously and continues to seduce her, knowing that he will not let her destroy him (138).

Each one of the men in Edna's life has a role in the novel. Her father has been the cause of repressing her emotions and leads her to make the wrong decision in marrying Mr. Pontellier. Mr. Pontellier is a kind and generous husband, but he is not the right husband for Edna. Edna remains self-contained until she spends the summer at Grand Isle. All the emotions that have been locked up within her now come forcefully to life as she awakens to her power as a woman. Robert watches her as she breaks free from all the social constraints that have been imprisoning her and understands the power she may have over him if he decides to stay; as a result, he leaves. He returns once more in her life only to run away again, leaving her a note that says, "I love you. Good-by—because I love you" (172). Arobin, on the other hand, takes advantage of Edna's awakening and is the only man who is able to approach Edna sexually and aggressively.

It is also important in the analysis of Edna as a femme fatale to take a close look at the two women who surround and influence Edna. Edna is surrounded and influenced by two women in the novel, Madame Ratignolle and Mademoiselle Reisz. Each of these women has a partial existence as a human being, the "Madame" being dedicated to her husband and children and "Madmoiselle" being dedicated solely to her music.

Adele Ratignolle is a woman who is attentive to her husband, children, and home. Chopin calls women of this type "mother-women" and describes them as

> fluttering around with extended, protecting wings when any harm, real or imaginary threatened their precious brood. They were women who idolized their children, worshipped their husbands, and esteemed it a holy privilege to efface themselves as individuals and grow wings as ministering angels. (51)

Madame Ratignolle's priorities are, according to the way Edna views them, self-constricting and leave no room for what Edna sees as a necessity—the inward life, an identity that is disconnected from being married and subjugated. In one of the most famous quotes of the novel, Edna explains to Adele, "I would give up the unessential; I would give my money. I would give my life to my children; but I wouldn't give myself" (97).

Edna observes Adele Ratignolle and sees how self-negating her life is. Adele Ratignolle is unable to perceive herself as an individual woman and possesses no sense of self beyond her role as a wife and mother. Edna watches how her friend's children adore her and how Adele returns their affection unconditionally, and unlike Edna, Adele Ratignolle "[thinks] about winter garments for her children" in the summer, while Edna "could not see the use of anticipating and making winter night garments the subject of her summer meditations" (60). Madame Ratignolle is a perfect example of a woman who has readily adopted the norms and values of the patriarchal domain and has readily accepted the traditional gender roles. Paradoxically, Edna also sees how self-negation runs parallel with marital happiness and social approval. This is evident in the scene of the dinner party that Edna throws herself on the occasion of her 29th birthday. When Monsieur Ratignolle talks about politics, city news, or even neighborhood gossip, "[H]is wife was keenly interested in everything he said, laying down her fork the better to listen, chiming in, taking the words out of his mouth," (145) yet never being able to fully articulate her own thoughts on any of the subjects her husband talks about. In this respect, Madame Ratignolle resembles the parrot that is introduced at the beginning of the story. She is a woman locked up in a cage, dully repeating the words and thoughts of her husband, yet never brave enough to speak the "language which no one understood."

In sharp contrast to the beautiful epitome of marital bliss stands the ugly, deformed, and lonely Mademoiselle Reisz, who lives solely for her art. She lives as an outcast, and few people (namely, Edna and Robert) in the novel can appreciate her music. Her music, for example, "sent a keen tremor down Mrs. Pontellier's spinal chord" (72). Yet, like Adele Ratignolle, Mademoiselle Reisz is wholly dedicated to her art, and is, therefore, unable to have a full existence as a human being. Her social life is insignificant, and almost everyone in the novel avoids being around her. Edna is the only person that develops a relationship with her, and Robert, the only other person sensitive to the Mademoiselle's music, corresponds with her via letters and explains to her the depth of his feelings toward the fatally attractive Edna.

Edna befriends both of these contradictory women in the novel and observes how each of these women lives. Each of the femme fatale figures discussed in this book so far is influenced by two other women in the novel who make decisions and choose paths for themselves. Trina mistakenly makes the choice of following in the footsteps of the reckless Maria Macapa instead of leading the dignified life of Miss Baker. Carrie watches her sister bury herself alive and would prefer to lead the life of the rich and graceful Mrs. Vance. Based on the two models Edna observes, Edna struggles to find a path she can follow. The mother-woman and the artist-woman, Showalter suggests,

> not only represent alternative roles and influences for Edna in the world of the novel, but...they also suggest different plots and conclusions. Adele's story suggests that Edna will give up her rebellion, return to her marriage, have another baby, and by degrees learn to appreciate, love, and even desire her husband...Mademoiselle Reisz's story suggests that Edna will lose her beauty, her youth,

her husband, and children—everything, in short, but her art and her pride. (*New Essays* 47)

Edna, however, perceives that both paths are unfulfilling and chooses neither path. Edna takes the road not taken, and seeks to appreciate love and desire, as Showalter puts it, but not for her husband, rather by being unfaithful to her husband and by seeking extramarital affairs that fulfill her desires to be wanted and to feel that she has power and autonomy. By doing so, Edna boosts her pride and overcomes the feeling of entrapment and the difficulties any naturalistic character feels locked up in a cage from which there is no escape. She denies partial existence as a mother and partial existence as an artist. In *Kate Chopin Reconsidered*, Martha Fodask Black argues that in denying the lifestyles of both women, Edna is forming herself into a New Woman:

> Although aroused by the older woman's music and envious of her freedom to pursue her artistic interests, Edna does not want to emulate Madmoiselle Reizs' life any more than she wants to accept a life like Adele's as a brood hen. Wishing for self-realization, Edna longs to design herself as a New Woman without being condemned to the role of the Victorian feminine. (111)

Yet, to read Edna as a New Woman is inadequate. Edna, like any New Woman, seeks social and economic independence and struggles to free herself of the patriarchal institution. In *The Awakening*, and unlike in *McTeague* and *Sister Carrie*, we witness the female protagonist defying gender and class conventions as she strives to achieve her personal freedom. Through a character like Edna, Chopin criticizes the position of women in American society at the turn of the twentieth century. It is beyond doubt that Edna does defy convention, but she does so only by asserting her individual preferences—having extramarital affairs, sexual in addition to social liberation and freedom. Edna's defiance of convention goes through many stages. After her sexual awakening, Edna is able, for the first time, to retort back at her husband: "Leonce, go to bed...I mean to stay out here. I don't wish to go in, and I don't intend to. Don't speak to me like that again; I shall not answer you" (78). Her verbal defiance strengthens her and enables her to desert her husband sexually. Her verbal defiance coupled with her sexual defiance leads to her economic independence. She frees herself completely from the dominance of her husband when she moves into her "pigeon-house." In a conversation with Madmoiselle Reisz, Edna explains the reason why she has decided to move out: "The house, the money that provides for it, are not mine...I have a little money of my own from my mother's estate...I won a large sum this winter on the races, and I am beginning to sell my sketches... I know I shall like it, like the feeling of freedom and independence" (134). Unlike Trina and Carrie, who feel that they need to get married in order to abide by the social conventions and to secure themselves financially as well, Edna gradually rids herself of the ties of marriage and seeks economic independence by making a living on her own. Thus, Edna's liberation of herself may seem as if she is becoming the New Woman of the twentieth century. She starts to make her own money and moves into a house to live by herself. In this respect, Edna is indeed freeing herself from the strong grip of patriarchal oppression.

Edna, however, does not provide an example of the New Woman who is ready to challenge the old century and make radical changes for the new century. Instead, Edna is the femme fatale created by American naturalism. Edna searches for power, but she only searches for self-power that helps her overcome heredity and environment. She is self-centered in her quest and does not demand or speak for women's rights. By being socially and economically independent, Edna is seeking emotional, psychological, and physical independence. Therefore, she becomes involved in adulterous affairs that empower her and make her feel that she is autonomous. Her quest is to liberate herself—but only to liberate herself—from the surrounding environment that she is locked in; she does not speak for the New Woman nor does she represent her. Susan K. Harris in *Nineteenth Century American Women's Novels* distinguishes Edna from other, better representatives of the New Woman and explains how fruitless Edna's quest is:

> Unlike Nan [Jewett's *A Country Doctor*], Edna has no specific purpose. Conscious of her restricted life, she, nevertheless drifts, rebelling against her limitation but unable to formulate concrete goals...She is awakened by a combination of music, sun, ocean, and a very pliable young man. Without a concrete force against which to define herself, her self-discovery is confused and aimless. (205)

Because Edna is self-centered in her quest, her motherhood also becomes questionable. In *McTeague*, Trina does not conceive and is denied motherhood because of her animalistic instints and her preoccupation with the gold she is saving. In *Sister Carrie*, Dreiser releases Carrie from the responsibilities of motherhood as a means of releasing Carrie from punishment and also for allowing her to pursue her acting career without the interference of children. However, Edna does have children—two boys. The message Chopin voices is clear: Edna is a woman and is destined in life to bear children. Moreover, by giving Edna two boys, Chopin is enveloping Edna with male presence and dominance. Edna's father, her husband, and her two boys are chaining her to the patriarchal prison.

Yet, despite the fact that Edna is a woman, she fails as a mother. One of the basic characteristics of the femme fatale figure is that she does not conceive, like Trina and Carrie for example, or if she does conceive, she can seldom carry out her responsibilities as a mother. This is typical of Edna, who, "in short, ...was not a mother-woman" (51). There are several instances in the novel that illustrate Edna's incapacity to be a mother-woman. These instances also help the reader understand how biological determinism in naturalism functions. Biology has helped determine Edna's destiny: Nature made her female and made her a mother as well. Nevertheless, Edna is rebelling against biological determinism. Paradoxically, she is a mother, yet she does not want to be a mother. Her ambivalence toward her children reflects her ambivalence toward her life and freedom:

> She was fond of her children in an uneven, impulsive way. She would sometimes gather them passionately to her heart; she would sometimes forget them...Their absence was a sort of relief, though she did not admit this. It seemed to free her of a responsibility which she had blindly assumed and for which Fate had not fitted her. (162)

As a femme fatale, Edna realizes that living for the sake of her children will consume her rather than endow her with life. Consequently, she seeks to endow herself with life by pursuing her own pleasures. In this way, instead of undergoing a process of self-denial that runs parallel with motherhood, Edna chooses the femme fatale path in which she can enjoy and assert her life.

Instead of sacrificing herself to her children, Edna chooses to live for herself.

McTeague, Sister Carrie, The Awakening: Trina, Carrie, and Edna

The gender of the writer plays a significant role in the construction of each one of the femmes fatales discussed so far in this book. In the creation of Trina and Carrie, Norris and Dreiser create femmes fatales but direct the readers' attention to the devastating effects the femmes fatales have on their male victims. We witness the male characters struggling with their uncontrollable sexual passions, and we witness their downfall because of the choices that they make. They blindly give in to the femmes fatales, allowing them to control them emotionally, economically, psychologically, and sexually. Kate Chopin, on the other hand, in her creation of Edna as femme fatale, does not place her emphasis on the passion of the male characters who surround Edna, but rather on Edna herself. We witness the femme fatale discovering her sexual power and struggling with her discovery. The passion of the female character is at the center of the work, and Chopin places the passions of the male characters in the background.

In *The Awakening*, the male characters who are under the spell of the femme fatale are seldom seen suffering with their passions. Edna's husband resumes his business after Edna chooses to leave his house and stays in touch with her by occasionally sending her letters. Likewise, Robert retreats from Edna's life, but instead of corresponding with Edna, he chooses to correspond with Madmoiselle Reisz and admits to her the nature of his passionate feelings toward Edna. Arobin pursues his relationship with Edna but is not depicted as a male who is passionate and sincere in his emotions toward Edna, and he will not, therefore, suffer because of his relationship with Edna.

Edna's passion is at the center of the novel. Edna experiences the power of her body in scenes that are private to the people around her but are made open to the reader. The scene in which Edna goes with Robert to the island of Cheniere and rests alone for some time at their friend's house is a typical example of her exploration of her body:

> Edna, left alone in the little sideroom, loosened her clothes, removing the greater part of them. She bathed her face, her neck, and her arms in the basin that stood between the windows. She took off her shoes and stockings and stretched herself in the very center of the high, white bed...She stretched her strong limbs that ached a little. She ran her fingers through her loosened hair for a while. She looked at her round arms as she held them straight up and rubbed them one after the other, observing closely, as if it were something she saw for the first time, the fine, firm quality and texture of her flesh. (84)

Unfortunately, Edna's realization of her power as a woman and the passion she has acquired for her sexual self brings about her own destruction and not the destruction of the men in her life.

Another difference between the representations of the femmes fatales in this study is that Trina and Carrie are depicted as greedy women whose main aim in attracting men is to secure themselves financially. Both Trina and Carrie struggle to acquire economic stability, and both become extremely greedy and selfish after they are able to do so. Edna, on the other hand, is depicted as a female who is struggling to rid herself of the riches she possesses and willingly strips herself of her marital status that provides her with economic stability. Chopin's message through a character like Edna is that Edna is not only seeking economic independence, but she is also seeking autonomy and spiritual independence, an idea explained by Joyce Dyer:

> That a woman might have both an active sexual life and an active spiritual life was incongruous to the nineteenth century. Yet Edna did. Briefly comparing Edna's attitude toward money with Trina's and Carrie's in *McTeague* (1899) and *Sister Carrie* (1900) establishes her spiritual superiority. All three women enjoy some degree of economic independence—the condition urged by Charlotte Perkins Gilman—but Edna shares neither Trina's obsession with money nor Carrie's understanding that it is linked to social ambition and success. Edna relies on the inheritance from her mother, as well as the money she makes from gambling at the races and her own painting, to purchase spiritual freedom. (15)

Moreover, given the fact that Edna is a woman created by a woman writer, Chopin chooses to give Edna children. This sets Edna apart from the other two femmes fatales, and "this points to a fundamental difference in emphasis: Kate Chopin concentrates mainly on the biological aspects of women's situation" (Seyersted 192). However, Edna does not carry out her responsibilities as a mother, unlike Adele Ratignolle, for example, and thinks of her children as obstructive to leading a carefree lifestyle. The fact that Edna does not function as a perfect mother-woman emphasizes the fact that Edna is another femme fatale who was created by American naturalism.

Yet these femmes fatales do share common ground despite their individual differences. In all the works discussed so far in this study, all three female protagonists assert their free will and find means of escaping the walled enclosures of heredity and environment. All three women use their beauty and sexual appeal to do so and are sending out a message that there is a means of escape. Despite the fact that all three characters eventually end up, nevertheless, crushed by heredity and environment, they have diligently tried to overcome.

In the cases of Carrie and Edna, both protagonists are neither condemned nor punished for their adulterous relationships. Both Dreiser and Chopin deal with women at the turn of the twentieth century who do not feel guilt nor remorse about committing adultery. Because of the fact that both works overstepped the moral conventions of their time, both novels were unacceptable to publishers and readers.

Although both novelists choose not to punish their female protagonists for their untraditional behavior, they do undergo a process of psychological suffering and misery. The female protagonists may seem like conquerors, but readers sense the female protagonists' loneliness, alienation, and boredom despite their victories. In *Sister Carrie*, Dreiser informs us:

> And now Carrie attained that which in the beginning seems like life's object, or, at least, such a fraction of it as human beings ever attain of their original desires. She could look about on her gown and carriage, her furniture, and her bank account. Friends there were...and yet she was lonely. (462)

The same state of being is seen in *The Awakening* in the dinner party which Edna gives for herself on the occasion of her 29th birthday:

> The golden shimmer of Edna's satin gown spread in rich folds on either side of her. There was a soft fall of lace encircling her shoulders. It was the color of her skin, without the glow, the myriad living tints that one may sometimes discover in the vibrant flesh. There was something in her attitude, in her whole appearance when she

leaned her head against the high-backed chair and spread her arms, which suggested the regal woman, the one who rules, who looks on, who stands alone. But as she sat there amid her guests, she felt the old ennui overtaking her, the hopelessness which so often assailed her. (145)

Toward the end of *McTeague*, Trina is brutally murdered by her victim. In the end of *Sister Carrie*, Carrie ends up as a dead-in-life character, sitting in her rocking chair, contemplating her place in the universe and realizing that her success on the stage is merely an act and that she has not been able to find true happiness and fulfillment. However, Edna chooses not to remain a dead-in-life female character after Robert abandons her for the second time, and in her last attempt to assert her free will, Edna chooses to take her own life.

Edna's Suicide
Edna Pontellier's suicide has received considerable attention and has been interpreted in several ways. On the one hand, some critics view Edna's death/suicide as a typical naturalistic ending of a naturalistic, fated character. Nancy Walker, for example, believes that Edna does not commit suicide but rather dies of natural causes: "Edna drifts into death because she does nothing to stop it...She has not controlled her destiny" (103). Similarly, George Arms views Edna's suicide as a passive drifting and asserts that she is the victim of her own self-delusion (215).

On the other hand, some critics view Edna's suicide as an act of self-assertion and as a transcendence of her earthly limitations. Donald Ringe describes Edna's death as a "defeat that involves no surrender" (588). Other critics focus on the ambiguous nature of the suicide. Edna does not compromise her vision of freedom; paradoxically, she is defeated by convention. Suzanne Wolkenfeld points out, "Edna's suicide is not a conscious choice reached through her achievement of self-awareness" (220). Margo Culley interprets Edna's drowning as a kind of liberation from the confining network of social relationships in which a woman is defined "as someone's daughter, someone's wife, someone's mother, someone's mistress" (288). And Joyce Dyer explains Edna's final act as a dramatization of "her mysterious understanding of a revolutionary concept of gender: [W]omen must be given recognition because of their worth as human-beings not because of their reproductive capacity" (101).

Edna's suicide calls for yet another interpretation in light of the femme fatale figure. In the process of awakening to her sexual power, Edna asserts her free will. Edna frees herself of the illusions of marriage, domesticity, and nineteenth-century womanhood. In addition, Edna frees herself of the illusions of motherhood. She also frees herself of the shame of adultery. Unfortunately, Edna also frees herself of the strong grip of life. Unable to cast a spell over Robert and unable to possess and control Robert, the femme fatale is defeated. She seeks to conquer Robert and realizes that, despite her victories, she remains defeated. As a result

> Edna walked on down to the beach rather mechanically, not noticing anything special except that the sun was hot. She was not dwelling upon any particular train of thought. She had done all the thinking which was necessary after Robert went away, when she lay awake upon the sofa till morning. (174–175)

Edna only chooses to end her life after Robert abandons her for the second time. She does not contemplate death as an option for her to break free, in any instance, before Robert leaves her for the second time, and she seeks to assert herself in every possible way in her new house and new profession. She chooses to deprive herself of life when she feels that she has failed repeatedly to entrap Robert. As a woman entering the twentieth century, Edna searches for definition and fulfillment through being recognized as a human being. As a femme fatale, Edna searches for definition and fulfillment through victimizing Robert. She fails to victimize and, consequently, ends her life. Thus, Edna is a female naturalistic character who strives to overcome the deterministic elements that control her life, who succeeds in some respects, and yet who fails in the role she takes as femme fatale. Edna overcomes pressures of environment and circumstance, overcomes forces that may seem beyond control for a nineteenth-century woman, yet fails to overcome Robert. In the case of Edna, the femme fatale becomes a victim of her own self. Edna swims into the open sea: "He [Robert] did not know: [H]e did not understand. He would never understand" (176).

CHAPTER 5

"It Had Begun, a New Life for Helga Crane:" Helga Crane as Femme Fatale in Nella Larsen's *Quicksand*

Published in 1928, Nella Larsen's novel *Quicksand* depicts a female protagonist who is struggling to find a true identity for herself because of her mixed ancestry. Because she is a mulatto, Helga Crane vainly searches for a sense of belonging. She moves from place to place, searching for something undefined and undefinable. Helga Crane is confined by both heredity and environment, and like the other female protagonists discussed so far, she finds no means of escape except by using her alluring charm and thus victimizing the men she encounters in her life. And, unfortunately, like the other female protagonists, Helga Crane is defeated. However, Helga Crane is distinctly different from the rest of the femmes fatales discussed in this study in that she is a mulatto and a woman who is living in the twentieth century. This chapter begins by explaining why this twentieth century novel by Nella Larsen is included in the study of American naturalism although the previous chapters have dealt with works written in the 1890's—the peak of the naturalistic movement. I shall offer an explanation of why this work in particular should be read as a typical naturalistic text. The chapter moves on to give a historical account of the Tragic Mulatto figure, placing particular emphasis on Helga Crane and her situation. The chapter examines Helga's background and environment, as well as her relationship with the men and the women she encounters, and explains why and how Helga Crane transforms herself from pursued to pursuer, thus becoming a femme fatale. Finally, the chapter offers an interpretation of the ending of the novel.

TWENTIETH-CENTURY AMERICAN NATURALISM

In *American Writing in the Twentieth Century*, Willard Thorp emphasizes, "[L]iterary naturalism refuses to die." He believes that the movement has the ongoing ability to renew itself decade after decade because of its "essential flexibility" (180). The flexibility that Thorp mentions is an idea that Pizer elaborates on in his book, *Twentieth Century Literary American Naturalism: An Interpretation*. Pizer explains what constitutes a naturalistic novel by emphasizing the themes with which the naturalistic novel mainly deals. One important theme in American naturalism is that of the waste of the individual potential because of the conditioning forces of life. Pizer argues, "[T]he naturalistic tragic hero is a figure whose potential for growth is evident but who fails to develop because of the circumstances of his life" (*Twentieth Century* 6). The second theme that Pizer emphasizes in American naturalism is the failure of the potentially undistinguished figure to maintain the order and stability that are essential in order to survive in a shifting, unstable world. The third naturalistic theme concerns the problem of the individual's knowledge. Pizer asserts, "Man is alone and doubtful in an unknown world of struggle, yet he searches in himself and in experience for confirmation of a traditional value" (*Twentieth Century* 7). The infrastructure for all the previously mentioned themes is the tragic incompleteness of life. Because of life's tragic incompleteness, a naturalistic tragic hero is both created in and needed for this literary movement:

> The American naturalistic hero is not a noble figure who falls from a high place and then discovers the reason for his fall. Because we are a society still committed to the dream of full development of each man's potential for the good life, we find it more moving to dramatize the crushing or blocking of the potential for fineness of mind and spirit than the loss of qualities already achieved...And because we have believed that certain truths are universal, permanent, and comprehensible, we are moved by the realization that we can seldom know anything than our own desires. (Pizer, *Twentieth Century* 8)

Moreover, the journey which the naturalistic tragic hero undertakes is circular with a return to the starting point, with little gained, achieved, or understood despite the tragic hero's movement through time and space.

This symbolic structure suggests that not only are human beings flawed and unfulfilled, but that experience itself does not guide or instruct human nature. While a vast skepticism with regard to the conventional attributes of experience is reflected within the naturalistic tradition, it should be noted that the naturalistic novel "affirms the significance and worth of the seeking temperament, of the character who continues to look for meaning in experience even though there is probably no meaning" (Pizer, *Twentieth Century* 9). In his article "Contemporary American Literary Naturalism," Pizer further argues,

> What has varied in the history of America is not the writer's commitment to the depiction of the inadequacies of American life itself. Rather it is the nature of American life itself—its particular social reality and intellectual preoccupations—that has changed and thereby resulted in varying themes and strategies of the American naturalistic novel. (*American* 256)

It is revealed that naturalism strongly persists within the pages of the novel by closely reviewing *Quicksand*, which was written in 1928. To be noted first is the title itself, which is suggestive of the human being's struggle for and within life itself. The entrapment and frustration of any naturalistic character can easily be applied to the concept of quicksand. Larsen's depiction of a sense of loss, struggle, fear, and horror in the life of Helga Crane is a typical depiction of a naturalistic character undergoing pressure both from her own free will and the crushing conditions of the society in which she is living. Larsen carefully provides us with an account of the earlier shaping environment of Helga Crane so that we may understand more clearly and thus justify the course of action she decides to pursue—that of the femme fatale. Larsen's work may well be read in the tradition of the naturalistic literary movement because she makes a milieu in which man/woman becomes a hunted, targeted, tortured being and because, for the most part, Helga Crane is determined by the pressures of not only her past, but also her present. Helga Crane has to cope with her heritage of mixed blood and, as a result, also has to endure the social malice she encounters because of her mixed blood. Helga Crane is an individual who does have the potential for growth. She is a woman with an educated background and with a career in teaching. Yet, her development is circumscribed because of the circumstances of her life. She drifts from one place to another, in the hope of finding the stability and order Pizer talks about, but she fails in her attempts. She is alone and unknown in a world of struggle; she does, nevertheless, search in herself and in experience for the "confirmation of a traditional value," (Pizer, *Twentieth Century* 7) which Pizer mentions, and which is a sense of belonging in the case of Helga Crane. Moreover, Helga undertakes a circular journey, a return to the starting point with little gained or understood despite her constant moving and shifting. The novel begins with Helga in the South, in Naxos. She moves to Chicago first and then to New York. She crosses the Atlantic and goes to Copenhagen, only to return to New York. Her circular journey ends in the South after she marries Reverend Green and returns to Alabama with him.

Thorp argues, "[M]odern philosophical naturalism avoids bleak determinism. It permits man a large measure of free will, operative in his own life and in the society in which he lives" (183). The idea of free will is manifested in the character of Helga Crane. Helga Crane is a woman who lives in the twentieth century, and the reader observes Helga living independently by herself, working because of her educational background, making firm, though rash, decisions, and moving freely and traveling about and even outside the continent without being obstructed or confined. She is operative in her own life and in the society in which she lives. She does exercise free will to a certain extent, but, unfortunately, she has to deal with the eternal problem of the color of her skin. Helga Crane is not limited by atavistic regression like Trina Sieppe; she is not limited by an industrial, materialistic society like Caroline Meeber; she is not limited by the paternal world like Edna Pontellier. Helga Crane is distinctly different from all the women discussed so far in this book; Helga Crane is a Tragic Mulatto figure.

The Plight of the Tragic Mulatto Figure

The Tragic Mulatto figure has been a pervasive figure in American literature in both the nineteenth and twentieth centuries. According to Judith Berzon, the Tragic Mulatto character is an "outcast, a wanderer, one alone. He is the fictional symbol of marginality" (100). Werner Sollors explains that the term Tragic Mulatto "normally refers to mainly descendants who constantly struggle with being neither black nor white" (223), and they are usually presented as people tormented by what Sollers calls "warring blood" (234). Nella Larsen's *Quicksand* provides an example of the Tragic Mulatto motif in the early twentieth century. Helga Crane is a lost, lonely figure because of her racial heritage. Hereditary and biological factors are inhibiting Helga Crane from finding true happiness and fulfillment wherever she goes. Because of the biological factors involved in Helga Crane's formation, we witness Helga Crane subjugated both internally with the thoughts of being a mulatto and externally with other people's thoughts about her being a mulatto.

Edward Byron Reuter explains how the intermixture of diverse racial elements produces the problems that are ever present in Helga Crane's life:

> It is not, then, the mere fact of a mixed ancestry that makes the mulatto a problem in the community and an object

of sociological interest. But when the crossing of races produces an offspring readily distinguishable from both the parent races of which it is a mixture, the situation becomes the basis for class distinctions; the bi-racial ancestry of the individual may determine his status in the community. (18)

Helga Crane's status in the community is that of a nonexistent entity with no particular purpose in life. The novel opens with a dreary image of loneliness and desolateness: "Helga Crane sat alone in her room which at that hour, eight in the evening, was in soft gloom." The shades of colors that Larsen skillfully depicts in the opening pages of the novel are reflective of the shades of colors that Helga Crane is suffering from, being like the "oasis in the desert of darkness" (1). The amalgamation of darkness, light, and shade in the beginning of the novel presents the reader with an understanding of the persisting inherited trait that creates a problem for Helga, that of being neither light nor dark, neither black nor white, yet living in a shade or shadow of both, affiliated with both colors, yet never belonging to either one, and as a result, "an observer would have thought her well-fitted to that framing of light and shade" (2).

Rueter also elaborates on the physical characteristics of the mulatto, asserting that mulattoes have

> [a] characteristic physical appearance [that] classifies them; it separates them from both groups, and makes them alien in both. It makes it impossible for them to escape the stigma which attaches itself to a tainted ancestry. The half-caste individual cannot, therefore, be a mere individual; he is inevitably the representative of a type. He is not merely a product; he is a sociological phenomenon. (19)

And as a result of being a sociological phenomenon, "psychologically, the mulatto is an unstable type" (Reuter 102). Helga

Crane's dissatisfaction with life is sensed from the beginning. After the reader is provided with a serene image of Helga in her room, Helga makes the unexpected, rash decision to leave her educational profession and to leave Naxos as well. She decides to leave "forever," stirring with "an overpowering desire for action of some sort" (4). Having determined to cease her persona as a teacher, Helga believes that she is undergoing some sort of rebirth, and the first chapter ends with her realization that the fact that she is in Naxos is related to the fact that she has been looking for a "social background, but—she could not have imagined that it could be so stuffy" (8). In addition to establishing the theme of the Tragic Mulatto, the first few chapters set out several important themes of the naturalistic novel. Helga struggles in the tension between free will and the obstructive forces of heredity and environment, and the tension between individuality and society and its establishments. Helga ponders her decision to leave and reassures herself, "[B]y an effort of will, her will, it could be done." Nevertheless, she hesitates:

> To remain seemed too hard. Could she do it? Was it possible in the present rebellious state of her feelings? The uneasy sense of being engaged with some formidable antagonist, nameless, and ununderstood, startled her. It wasn't, she was suddenly aware, merely the school and its way and its decorous stupid people that oppressed her. There was something else, some other ruthless force, a quality within herself, which was frustrating her, had always frustrated her, kept her from getting the things she had wanted. Still wanted. (11)

In her attempt to run away from her past ambivalent heritage, the first strategy Helga Crane adopts is to move from one place to another. Helga meets with Dr. Anderson, the school principal where she is working at Naxos, who "for some reason she had liked" (23). She explains to Dr. Anderson, "[Her] father was a gambler who deserted [her] mother, a white immigrant. It is even uncertain that they were married" (21). After Dr. Anderson fails to convince Helga to stay, she determinedly leaves Naxos and everything related to Naxos, including her fiancée, James Vayle. And like Carrie, Helga finds herself in the big, industrial, merciless city of Chicago, seeking a relative and with little money in her possession. During her lonely, tiresome journey on the train, we learn more about her past circumstances. Her mother, "a fair Scandinavian girl in love with life, with love, with passion," risked everything "all in one blind surrender." Helga's father deserted her mother soon afterward and the mother was "flung into poverty, sordidness, and dissipation." Helga's mother remarried "a man of her own race," with the result of complete neglect of Helga, until Helga's mother died when Helga was 15. Helga was sent to a school for Negroes under the recommendation of her uncle, Peter Nilssen, where "for the first time she could breathe freely, where she discovered that because one was dark, one was not necessarily loathsome, and could, therefore, consider oneself without repulsion." Yet, for Helga Crane, "there had been always a feeling of strangeness, of outsidedness, and of one holding her breath for fear that it wouldn't last" (23). These thoughts that she is having on the train show how entrapped and frustrated Helga is with her past. Helga's journey to Chicago takes her back to her birthplace and causes her to experience "a queer feeling of enthusiasm" (30), yet paradoxically, this journey causes her much agony and heartbreak when she has to face her past once again.

In Chicago, Helga decides to ask Uncle Peter for assistance, although "she detested her errand" (27). Upon meeting Uncle Peter's wife for the first time, Helga faces another encounter with her past. Mrs. Nilssen speaks sharply with Helga and reminds her that she has no home and no family in Chicago, bluntly stating, "You mustn't come here any more...And please remember that my husband is not your uncle" (28–29). This episode reminds Helga that kinship ties are weaker than the ties of racial identity. When Helga explains to Mrs. Nilssen that she is Mr. Nilssen's neice, Mrs. Nilssen "plainly wished to dissociate herself from the outrage of [Helga's] very existence" (29). Helga, who comes to her birthplace in search of a feeling of belonging, realizes the fruitlessness of her visit to her uncle's house and to Chicago: "And, oddly enough, she felt, too, that she had come home. She, Helga Crane, who had no home" (30).

Her later plight in Chicago echoes Sister Carrie's vain search for a job and a means of making an honest living there. Both female protagonists admire money and the beautiful things they can buy if they have enough money. Both seek help from blood relatives but face the cold reality of the insignificance of blood relations in the face of stronger issues. Carrie should not expect to be welcomed unless she can contribute to the living expenses of her sister's household. Helga Crane is not even welcome because of the mixed blood running in her veins. Both women are sincere and honest in their quests in the beginning, yet Carrie easily succumbs to temptation and engages in a disguised form of prostitution as a means of living a comfortable life in the big city of Chicago. To Helga Crane, after having failed to find a decent job that matches her education and intellectuality, prostitution is an option:

> Days of this sort of thing. Weeks of it. And the futile scanning and answering of newspaper advertisements. She traversed acres of streets, but it seemed that in that whole energetic place, nobody wanted her services. At least not the kind she offered. A few men, both white and black, offered her money, but the price of money was too dear. Helga Crane did not feel inclined to pay it. (34)

Helga is, nevertheless, adamant in her refusal at this early point in the novel to give in to temptation and to use her sexual appeal to find a means of living and of feeling secure.

Helga Crane's suffering in Chicago ends when she finds employment with Mrs. Hayes-Bore, "a prominent race woman and authority on the problem," and travels to New York with her (38). In New York, Helga experiences firsthand the Harlem Renaissance, where "the migration of thousands of blacks from the rural South to northern cities reflected and produced a renewed race consciousness and pride" (Wall, *Women* 1). Helga is introduced to Anne Grey and is satisfied for a period of time: "Thus established, secure, comfortable, Helga soon became thoroughly absorbed in the distracting interests of life in New York" (45). In Harlem, Helga meets people who share her tastes and ideas. She briefly feels a sense of freedom in Harlem; she is accepted there and becomes convinced that Harlem offers a completely satisfying life for her: "and she was satisfied, unenvious. For her, this Harlem was enough" (45).

However, the more time Helga spends with Anne Grey and her friends, the more Helga starts to see that these black people who are possessed of a race consciousness are themselves proud, superficial, insensitive, and hypocritical. They seem to immerse themselves in the race problem and speak out for the rights of black people, yet, at the same time, these people imitate the lifestyle, the values, and the ways of life of the white people. The paradoxicality and duality of the Harlemites are exemplified in Anne Grey, who "hated white people with a deep and burning hatred, with the kind of hatred which, finding itself held in sufficiently numerous groups, was capable some day, on some great provocation, of bursting into dangerously malignant flames." Simultaneously, Anne Grey "aped their [white people's] clothes, their manners, and their gracious way of living. While proclaiming loudly the undiluted good of all things Negro, she yet disliked the songs, the dances, and the softly blurred speech of the race" (48).

To Helga, Anne Grey is the epitome of hypocrisy and duality. Audrey Denney, on the other hand, a woman whom Anne Grey disdains, is true to her nature and true to herself. Like all the other female protagonists discussed in this study, Helga watches the life styles and strategies of two women in dealing, in this case, with the particular problem of the color of their skin and has to decide which lifestyle she would like to follow. Anne Grey is not true to herself or to her race; Audrey Denney is. In the scene when Helga expresses her admiration for the daring, self-assured Audrey Denney, Helga starts thinking about taking Audrey's course of action. Like Helga, Audrey is a mulatta, affiliated neither with the blacks nor with the whites, but encumbered by the norms that define black women. And like Helga, Audrey is an attractive young woman. Audrey, however, realizes that the only way of fighting the societal boundaries created between the two races is, in fact, to mix with the two races and to use her mystifying sexual appeal. Audrey is a typical femme fatale who influences Helga Crane:

> She [Audrey] was pale, with a peculiar, almost deathlike pallor. The brilliantly red, soft, curving mouth was somehow sorrowful. Her pitch-black eyes, a little aslant, were veiled by broad brows, which seemed like black smears. The short dark hair was brushed severely back from the wide forehead. (60)

Audrey Denney chooses to transgress the societal boundaries of the black race, much to the disdain of Anne Grey. Helga tries to question Anne about the course of action Audrey Denney dares to undertake, but Anne refuses to engage in a fair, intellectual conversation, leaving Helga to go home feeling "cold, unhappy, misunderstood, and forlon" (62). Helga's admiration for Audrey Denney stems from her own need to express her sexuality and to be able to mingle not only with the black race, not only with the white race, but rather with both. Helga would very much like to be like Audrey but lacks, at this point, the courage to do so.

Gradually, Helga Crane comes to understand the coexistence of "vice and goodness, sadness and gayety, ignorance and wisdom, ugliness and beauty, poverty and richness" in Harlem. Helga's own difficulties in defining herself arise from the duality and the coexistence of black and white, and she finally acknowledges the fact that life in New York does not fulfill her. She begins to feel that the place is suffocating her, and instead of experiencing the consciousness and pride of her race, Helga "made lonely excursions to places outside of Harlem" (47), until she finally decides to leave for Copenhagen: "It had begun, a new life for Helga Crane" (66).

Because of her different skin color, Helga Crane is welcomed with open arms in Denmark. Rueter explains that due to the fact that mulattoes are of a divergent type, they "excite interest and curiosity; they may even enjoy a prestige simply by virtue of their unlikeliness" (319). Helga once again feels that she has found a home, this time with white people, not black. Ironically, Helga is escaping from her past heritage yet finds refuge in her relations from the past. Ironically, Helga is running away from her colored skin yet is welcomed in Denmark because of her colored skin. And ironically, Helga feels a sense of belonging with the white race in Denmark exactly like the sense of belonging she first felt with the black race when she was in Harlem: "This [Denmark], then, was where she belonged. This was her proper setting. She felt consoled at last for the spiritual wounds of the past" (67). She finally feels rewarded for being a mulatto and is satisfied with all the attention and admiration instead of the indignation and disrespect that she has previously been accustomed to: "[S]he liked the small murmur of wonder and admiration which rose when Uncle Poul brought her in. She liked the compliments in the men's eyes as they bent over her hand. She liked the subtle half-understood flattery of her dinner partners" (70).

However, like every other place Helga goes to, she soon realizes that she does not belong in Denmark, and because of this lack of sense of belonging, her happiness does not last very long. The naturalistic theme of the strong grip of the past is persistent in Helga's life. In the South, she does not feel affiliated with her race. She travels north and feels that she does not belong there either. She travels abroad and feels accepted until she attends a circus where "two black men, American Negroes undoubtedly," perform and dance for the Scandinavian audience who applaud enthusiastically once the performance is over. At that point, she realizes that she, too, has been a spectacle for the white people to applaud and admire:

> Helga Crane was not amused. Instead she was filled with a fierce hatred for the cavorting Negroes on the stage. She felt shamed, betrayed, as if these pale pink and white people among whom she lived had suddenly been invited to look upon something in her which she had hidden away and wanted to forget. (83)

Once she understands that she is welcome only because of her difference, Helga confesses to herself: "I'm homesick, not for America, but for Negroes. That's the trouble" (92). Helga Crane thus decides to return to New York.

Helga Crane's Liberation

Amidst all the journeys that Helga Crane is undertaking, the femme fatale spirit gradually overtakes her way of thinking. Like

Sister Carrie and Edna Pontellier, who were not born as femmes fatales, but were rather created as femmes fatales because of the surrounding circumstances, Helga Crane starts to understand that the only power she has in her possession is, paradoxically, the one thing that is ostracizing her from society—her charming and mystifying physical appearance and beauty:

> A slight girl of [22] years, with narrow, sloping shoulders and delicate but well-turned arms and legs, she had, none the less, an air of radiant, careless health. In vivid green and gold negligee and glistening brocaded mules, deep sunk in the big high-backed chair, against whose dark tapestry her sharply cut face, with skin like yellow satin, was distinctly outlined, she was...attractive. Black, very broad brows over soft, yet penetrating, dark eyes, and a pretty mouth, whose sensitive and sensuous lips had a slight questioning petulance and a tiny dissatisfied droop, were the features on which the observer's attention would fasten; though her nose was good, her ears delicately chiseled, and her curly blue-black hair plentiful and always straying in a little wayward, delightful way. (2)

Helga Crane has charmed many men because of her distinctive beauty. James Vayle, the son of prominent black Atlantans, is her fiancée in the beginning of the novel. There are many drawbacks to their relationship, but the biggest drawback is that Helga has white blood and a questionable background: "She was, she knew, in a queer indefinite way, a disturbing factor. She knew too that a something held him, a something against which he was powerless. The idea that she was in but one nameless way necessary to him filled her with a sensation amounting almost to shame." But it is this same drawback that makes Helga powerful: "And yet his mute helplessness against that ancient appeal by which she held him pleased her and fed her vanity—gave her a feeling of power" (8).

The feeling of power which Helga Crane has over men intensifies
the more frustrated she becomes with her life as she becomes more
and more alienated and cut off from society. In Chicago, after her
encounter with Mrs. Nilssen, "it was as if all the bogies and gob-
lins that had beset her unloved, unloving, and unhappy childhood, had come to life with tenfold power to hurt" (29). In New
York, upon her second encounter with Dr. Anderson, "again,
abruptly had come the uncontrollable wish to wound" (51). In
Denmark, Axel Olsen, like McTeague and Hurstwood, cannot
resist the temptation of the femme fatale and confesses to Helga
how captivated and intrigued he is by her charm: "I…cannot
hold out against the deliberate lure of you. You disturb me. The
longing of you does harm to my work. You creep into my brain
and madden me" (86). Upon hearing this, Helga is satisfied from
within because of the power she feels she has over him; nevertheless, she coldly responds: "But you see, Herr Olsen, I'm not
for sale. Not to you. Not to any white man. I don't at all care to
be owned. Even by you" (87).

The feelings Helga has to wound and to conquer reach their
peak when Helga is back in New York. Instead of being victimized, Helga decides to become the victimizer; instead of being
pursued, Helga decides to become the pursuer; instead of being
pitiful, Helga decides to be vindictive. Helga Crane becomes the
typical femme fatale figure once she returns to New York:

> And Helga, since her return, was more than ever popular
> at parties. Her courageous clothes attracted attention, and
> her deliberate lure—as Olsen had called it—held it. Her
> life in Copenhagen had taught her to expect and accept
> admiration as her due. This attitude, she found, was as
> effective in New York as across the sea. It was, in fact,
> even more so. And it was more amusing too. Perhaps
> because it was somehow a bit more dangerous. (98)

Thus, Helga becomes an imminent danger to men, and her friend Anne Grey notices and acknowledges the fact that Helga does have destructive powers that may disrupt her marriage:

> [Anne] was sure that her marriage could be managed by tact and a little cleverness on her part. She was truly fond of Helga, but seeing how she had grown more charming, more aware of her power, Anne wasn't so sure that her sincere and urgent request to come over for her wedding hadn't been a mistake. (95)

Helga attends parties and social gatherings upon her return to New York with the intention of being disruptive. Incidentally, the two men Helga is connected to in the beginning of the novel in the South reappear toward the end of the novel in the North. Whereas Cheryl Wall believes that the reappearance of these men in the Harlem sequences demonstrates that "the expectations for women remain the same" no matter where the women go or what they do (Wall, *Women* 99), I believe that the reappearance of these men serves another function. In the beginning of the novel, these men are the victimizers and are the controllers who make Helga, the mulatta, feel unwelcome, insignificant, and different from the pure black race, and who are responsible for making Helga feel like a subordinated figure in a ruthless society. In the end of the novel, both Dr. Anderson and James Vayle reappear in a different guise. Because of Helga's transformation into a femme fatale, these men become the insignificant, helpless prey of the femme fatale. Helga rejoices to see James Vayle still recovering from the fact that she has left him, still longing to be with her: "Inwardly, she grinned, flattered. He hadn't forgotten. He was still hurt" (100). He asks her for the second time to marry him, and Helga "was very sorry for James Vayle," and she carelessly walks away from him and goes "tripping off with a handsome coffee-colored youth whom she had beckoned from across the room with a little smile" (104).

That same night, Helga encounters Anne's new husband, Dr. Anderson who, suddenly, kisses her passionately until the two of them feel "a long-hidden, half-understood desire welled up...with the suddenness of a dream" (104). Weeks after the kiss takes place, Dr. Anderson asks Helga to meet with him alone. Mistakenly, Helga feels that this is the moment when she can exercise her free will as a woman and more important as a femme fatale. However, the scene ends with an angry slap on the face of Dr. Anderson. The femme fatale is denied the opportunity to culminate this affair and she is denied the opportunity to control this man.

Charles Larson offers an interpretation of Helga and the men she encounters in her life:

> The men in Helga's life do not particularly help her understand her situation, though in no way can they be considered her major problem...The problem is Helga herself: her restlessness, her feelings of superiority, her deeply rooted sense of insecurity about her blackness, all the seemingly contradictory aspects of her personality. Self-hatred can manifest itself in many ways, and certainly one of the most common is to disdain everyone else. (73)

Not only is Helga manifesting her anger by showing contempt and disdain for the men in her life, she is also manifesting her anger and taking revenge on the whole world by trying to conquer these men. Dr. Anderson, like Robert Lebrun, understands the consequences of getting involved with the femme fatale and realizes the ramifications it may have on his marriage to Anne Grey; therefore, he chooses to retreat. The fact that he does not allow Helga to control him leads Helga, like Edna Pontellier, to her self-destructive end.

The ending of the novel signifies the defeat of the femme fatale. Like all other femmes fatales discussed in this study, Helga Crane loses her battle. Helga Crane mistakenly seeks refuge in marriage. The femme fatale does not have the opportunity to culminate the relationship with any of the men she encounters, and desperately finds a means of doing so by marrying Reverend Green. Deborah McDowell explains the decision that Helga makes in terms of its legitimacy:

> The only condition under which sexuality is not shameless is if it finds sanction in marriage. Further, because she is born out of wedlock, Helga is preoccupied with the issue of "legitimacy." Marriage to a preacher, is, then, legitimacy doubled. (xxi)

Helga Crane, however, is not preoccupied with legitimacy. What she is occupied with at the point she meets the Reverend is culminating an affair and thus having the sense of victory she has not been able to feel with Dr. Anderson. Back in Copenhagen, Helga is preoccupied with legitimacy up to the point when Axel Olsen proposes to her and before she decides to follow in the footsteps of the carefree Audrey Denney. In Copenhagen, when Axel Olsen takes an interest in her, it is solely physical: "Superb eyes...color...neck column...yellow...hair...alive... wonderful" (71).

As Helga spends more time with Axel, she becomes aware of his increasing interest in her. Helga, to him, is a mysterious physical object of beauty which leaves him no option but to wonder at her. She realizes that he is not by any means interested in her intellectuality, but rather, he is very much interested in her sexual and dangerous beauty. During the process of painting Helga, he candidly explains to her that he expects her to enter into a sexual relationship with him, not a marriage. This is when

Helga is still occupied with legitimacy. She calls Axel Olsen's suggestion ungentlemanly and an insult to "decent girls" such as herself.

Axel Olsen's portrait of Helga is not only "a metaphor... pertinent to Helga's struggle throughout the novel" (Miller 124). In drawing the portrait, Axel sees the darker side of Helga. He is able to see the femme fatale spirit within Helga and bravely informs her "You have the warm impulsive nature of the women of Africa, but, my lovely, you have, I fear, the soul of a prostitute. You sell yourself to the highest bidder" (87). Olsen, according to Miller, "perceives Helga as an entity consisting of two disparate halves and depicts the half he finds most alluring" (125). Helga refutes the truth of his representation: "It wasn't, she contended, herself at all, but some disgusting, sensual creature with her features." But later in New York, Helga understands that Axel Olsen has been able to probe deep into her mentality and predict the future she will choose for herself, a future in which her sensuality will overcome her intellectuality and lead her to be like Audrey Denney, a femme fatale who is not by any means preoccupied with legitimacy. Eventually, she admits to herself, "[Her picture] is, after all, the true Helga Crane" (89). Axel Olsen's reproduction of Helga as a sexual object in the painting becomes a reality when Helga returns to New York and is triggered by Dr. Anderson's kiss. At that point, Helga abandons all claims of legitimacy and makes the decision to indulge in a sexual affair: "[S]he had mentally prepared herself for the coming consummation; physically too, spending hours before the mirror" (107).

In her choice to marry Reverend Green, Helga is concerned with fulfilling her long repressed sexual desire and is also expressing her anger for not being able to victimize Dr. Anderson. Her decision is made instantaneously, without much contemplation: "Helga Crane had deliberately stopped thinking" (116). Finally, the picture that Axel Olsen draws is able to come to life. After she is repulsed by Dr. Anderson, the sexual desires in Helga have reached their peak. She longs to articulate a self which is liberated from all forms of repression, desire, and need. Although her choice in marrying the Reverend is a tragic one, she, at least, has been able to fulfill the sexual desires raging within her.

Helga marries the Reverend and returns in her cyclical journey to the South again. However, the sexual happiness, fulfillment, and most important, dominance she has been looking for as a femme fatale are nowhere to be found within this marriage. Her marriage becomes synonymous with pain, misery, and childbearing. Helga Crane is punished for her decision to entrap the Reverend, and instead of having control over the relationship, she finds that she has no control over the marriage and over her body. Marriage, pregnancy, and childbearing suffocate her. Helga's end reiterates Edna's position on the institution of marriage as an obstructive force in a woman's development. Edna chooses to overthrow this force; Helga chooses to accept it. Thus, marriage becomes the force that leads the femme fatale to death in life in the case of Helga Crane. Instead of finding happiness and stability, marriage provides Helga with an increased sense of dissatisfaction with herself and with her body. In this respect, "Larsen dismantles the myth that marriage elevates women in the social scale; she suggests that for them the way up, is ironically and paradoxically, the way down" (McDowell xxi).

By gradually losing control of her body and her mind, Helga loses control of her free will. In her choice to marry the Reverend and bear his children, motherhood becomes another naturalistic source of entrapment from which there can be no possible means of escape. All her previous notions of refusing to get married and bear children in order to save them from the kind of life that she herself has experienced vanish, indicating how little control Helga eventually has over her life. The color of her skin becomes not the only problem from which she can find no means of escape. Her children further entrap her and create a prison from which she can never escape. In addition to being a naturalistic theme, childbearing can also be seen as the punishment of the femme fatale.

In the construction of the female protagonists discussed so far in this book, motherhood, or the lack of motherhood, has its connotations. In *McTeague*, part of Trina's punishment for being a femme fatale is depriving her of motherhood. In *Sister Carrie*, Carrie does not have children from any of the illegitimate affairs she indulges in as a means of subverting the traditional punishment associated with carrying on illegitimate affairs. In *The Awakening*, Edna Pontellier, created by a woman author, has children as an indication of the prescribed role for women. In *Quicksand*, Helga Crane is punished by constant childbearing, and the image of quicksand becomes very clear in the very last lines of the novel: "And hardly had she left her bed and become able to walk again without pain, hardly had the children returned from the homes of the neighbors, when she began to have her fifth child" (135). The two female protagonists who do have children, Edna and Helga, fail as mothers—a role that is not prescribed for the typical femme fatale figure. Edna deserts her children; Helga contemplates this option: "It was so easy and so pleasant to think about freedom and cities," but she faces the unanswered questions: "How, then, was she to escape from the oppression, the degradation, that her life had become? It was so difficult. It was terribly difficult. It was almost hopeless" (135). Nella Larsen closes the novel with the repeated image of quicksand: Helga Crane has imposed upon her children the curse that she herself has been living with all her life—that of being a Tragic Mulatto.

Literary critics have emphasized the tragic end of Helga Crane and have explained it in terms of her mixed ancestry. Conscious of the color of her skin, Helga Crane feels alienated, foreign, and marginal wherever she goes—her mother's home, Devon, Naxos, her uncle's home, New York, Copenhagen, and finally Alabama. This lack of connectedness has its ramifications. In her lifelong struggle to figure out who she is, to whom she belongs, and how she can relate to other people, Helga Crane drifts aimlessly from one place to another. She finally believes that she can find happiness and a true identity for herself by asserting her sexuality and making use of her sexual appeal. She fails to do so with Dr. Anderson and ends up as the wife of Reverend Green. Larson contends, "[T]he grim ending implies that educated black women—sophisticated and cultured black women, middle-class black women—are trapped in life with no satisfactory alternatives" (72). Miller asserts the tragic end of Helga and explains it in terms of the dichotomies that are persistent in Helga's life:

> While Helga longs to articulate a self liberated from old forms, she can never quite verbalize a self or a world outside of the rigid dichotomies offered to her: Negro/white, America/Europe, spiritual freedom/physical freedom. The predicament in which she finds herself at the end of the novel exemplifies another in a series of situations in which her warring desires lead her to a relationship that confines rather than liberates. (126)

On the other hand, McDowell asserts, "[T]he issue of female sexuality dominates the novel" (xvii). In addition to the fact that female sexuality is a pivotal point in the novel, it is my opinion that the problems of the Tragic Mulatto are fully exposed in the character of Helga Crane. The conflicts which arise from

Helga's obscure past are haunting. Wherever she goes, she finds temporary sustenance and relief until her happiness is thwarted by her surrounding environment, which leads her to deliberately ostracize herself. She is entrapped physically, psychologically, intellectually, and socially. After she understands that the attention she has been receiving in Copenhagen is the same thing from which she is running away, she mistakenly believes that sexual fulfillment will bring her the happiness and stability she has been searching for all her life. She becomes daring and threatening and is finally able to wear the clothes and colors that are typically associated with the femme fatale. Her sexual desires are inherent and finally explode with the rejection of Dr. Anderson. I assert that Helga's sexual desires are not sexual desires per se. Helga believes that she can take vengeance on the world that has created her as a mulatta by asserting her sexual power, thus becoming the victimizer instead of the victim. By becoming a femme fatale, Helga believes she can escape heredity and environment and, at the same time, can manifest her anger and take revenge. Unfortunately, Helga Crane's end is indeed a tragic one, tragic because of Helga's wrongful attitude and fatal decisions. Unlike Edna who commits suicide, Helga Crane's suicide is like Carrie's: psychological. The femme fatale is defeated and conquered instead of being the conqueror. Like Trina who is murdered by McTeague, like Carrie whose life becomes meaningless despite her success, and like Edna who chooses to end her own life, Helga ends up in a state of emotional and physical collapse, longing to have her unmarried life back, but ultimately paying the price for the choice(s) she has made.

CHAPTER 6

EXAMPLES OF OTHER
FEMMES FATALES
IN AMERICAN NATURALISM

In American naturalism, male as well as female characters have been perceived as "pawns driven by outer forces or inner urges" that have been denied free will and are the victims of forces beyond their control (Ahnebrink 28). This book has aimed to show that women in American naturalism in particular are, nevertheless, able to make choices, to deliberate before they act, after having considered among a full array of motives and desires. This study suggests that women in American naturalism resist socioeconomic pressures and take control, to some extent, of their lives by becoming femmes fatales.

This book has aimed to show that the femme fatale of American naturalism is a distinctive kind of femme fatale. She is fabricated and reconstructed according to the needs of this literary movement. American naturalism has created a different version of the femme fatale. The femmes fatales of American naturalism are not like "La Belle Dame Sans Marci," and neither are the men who fall as their victims like the kings, princes, warriors, and knights that fall under the spell of the supernatural femme fatale. The femme fatale of American naturalism begins as a downtrodden, weak woman who falls as the victim of heredity and environment. She is neither powerful nor endowed with supernatural powers. She is the victim who has little power over her surrounding circumstances until she realizes that power exists within her own self—the power of her femininity and charm. In order to fight heredity and environment, the femme fatale of American naturalism ends up using her sexuality as her only means of escape.

This book has aimed to prove that the femme fatale is not only a timeless archetype, but also the product of a literary movement that shows woman caught in a net from which there can be no easy means of escape. This book has also aimed to prove that women in American naturalism are more types than individuals. Trina, Carrie, Edna, and Helga are all alike in that they have all suffered injustice in one form or another. They are also alike in that they have all fought back and driven themselves to desperate ends.

The man in American naturalism is also the victim of heredity and environment, but he can also fall prey to the femme fatale. Despite the shortcomings in their lives, both McTeague and Hurstwood are content until they encounter Trina and Carrie. Once these femmes fatales enter their lives, their downfalls begin. Because Trina and Carrie are femmes fatales created by male writers, emphasis is placed on the degeneration and downfall of the male characters who fall under their spells. In *The Femme Fatale Myth: Sources and Manifestations in Selected Visual Media 1880–1920,* Edward Farrell asserts that the femme fatale is a disruptive, as well as destructive, force in the life of the men she encounters. The femme fatale, who is "a symbol of carnality and sensuousness," can "rob men of their home life, their health, and their reason; she was believed to reduce man to the level of beasts" (18). This is precisely what happens with McTeague and Hurstwood, who become pitiful and hopeless men who eventually beg for love, support, and money from the cold, heartless femme fatale.

In *The Awakening* and *Quicksand,* the female authors lay more emphasis on the suffering of the femme fatale herself than on the suffering of the men that these femmes fatales encounter. The reader witnesses Edna as she awakens to her sexual power and witnesses Robert Lebrun as he makes the deliberate choice of staying away from the woman who has awakened to her sexuality. Edna's suffering is at the center of the work, and little is mentioned about Lebrun's suffering. Similarly, Helga Crane chooses to use her sexuality as her last resort in an attempt to make up for her lack of sense of belonging and to escape from the color of her skin. And similarly, the reader is made more aware of Helga's suffering than of the suffering of James Vayle, Dr. Anderson, or Axel Olsen.

The women discussed in this book share common ground despite their individual differences. Farrell explains how a late-nineteenth-century woman may be "tagged" as a femme fatale. A woman might be considered a femme fatale if she poses or appears nude, if she flaunts her wealth and personality or holds a radical political position, or if she becomes an actress, an artist's model, or a prostitute. A woman might also be looked at as a femme fatale if she becomes involved in any kind of publicly scandalous activity, or if she lives out of wedlock with a man, if she is divorced, if she drinks, smokes cigarettes, or bobbs her hair, or if she inspires jealousy in men or women (17).

All the women discussed in this book engage in one or more of the actions mentioned by Farrell that are typically associated with the femme fatale figure. Carrie ponders her situation before she makes the transition from Drouet to Hurstwood: "How was it that, in so little a while, the narrow life of the country had fallen from her as a garment, and the city, with all its mystery, taken its place?" (124). Selling herself is her means of escape from the merciless industrial world in which she finds herself. Carrie also becomes a successful actress. Edna Pontellier does not engage in prostitution, but she does become involved in a scandalous situation. In her attempt to liberate herself from the control of her husband, Edna resolves to leave her husband's household and chooses to live by herself in the "pigeon-house." Edna also drinks freely at dinner parties. Moreover, Edna becomes involved with two other men while she is still the wife of Mr. Pontellier. Helga Crane poses for Axel Olsen to draw her. Helga also welcomes the idea of becoming involved with Dr. Anderson, a married man, and is on the verge of becoming involved in a scandalous situation. Trina inspires jealousy in Marcus; Carrie inspires jealousy in both Drouet and Hurstwood; Edna inspires jealousy in both Robert and Arobin; Helga inspires jealousy in Anne Grey, Dr. Anderson, and James Vayle.

Thus, this study is a work of synthesis; it emphasizes the similarities among the femmes fatales, although each femme fatale was created under different circumstances. It is a synthetic study of the femme fatale as seen throughout the American naturalistic movement. The American naturalistic femme fatale's use of her sexuality involves a complex matrix of human psychopathology, sexuality, and economics. In various situations, the femme fatale's use of her sexual appeal and distinctive beauty may involve the need to survive, as in Carrie, the drive for wealth, as in Trina, the drive for power and control, as in Edna, or the drive for (self) punishment, as in Helga.

The femme fatale is a persistent figure that appears in a number of other American naturalistic texts. In addition to the women discussed in this book, I will briefly mention a few other examples of femmes fatales in American naturalism. Stephen Crane, one of the leading American naturalists, created *Maggie, a Girl of the Streets*, in 1893. The story of Maggie is similar to the stories of the women discussed in this book in that she is living in a victimizing world. The dreadful life she is living leads her to prostitution and eventually to committing suicide. As with Carrie, Maggie's decision to sell herself is the direct result of her surrounding environment, and like Carrie, Maggie has urgent desires to become rich and be well-dressed, realizing that working in a factory will not give her the kind of life for which she wishes: "She [Maggie] began to note, with more interest, the well-dressed women she met on the avenues. She envied elegance and soft palms. She craved those adornments of person which she saw every day on the street, conceiving them to be allies of vast importance to women" (35). After leaving her dreary household to be with Pete, her brother's friend, Maggie mistakenly believes that she has found the happiness that she has been searching for, and she also mistakenly believes that being with Pete is her way out of the suffocating naturalistic environment within which she is trapped: "At times Maggie told Pete long confidential tales of her former home life, dwelling upon the escapades of the other member of the family and the difficulties she had had to combat in order to obtain a degree of comfort" (55). However, her happiness with Pete does not last very long, and she comes to the realization that she has been entrapped in another victimizing world that has no pity on her as a human being. She aimlessly returns home, but having no kind of moral support from her mother and brother, Maggie is driven to commit suicide once Pete abandons her.

Harold Fredrick's *The Damnation of Theron Ware* tells the story of the decline and fall of a Methodist minister. Literary critics place particular emphasis on the fall of the minister, but do not emphasize one of the reasons behind his fall. By enchanting the minister with the music she plays on the organ, Celia Madden, another example of a femme fatale figure in American naturalism who is "bold" and has a "luxuriant quality of…beauty," (140) plays a major role in the degradation and damnation of Theron Ware.

In 1919, Sherwood Anderson published *Winesburg, Ohio*, a novel that includes related short sketches and tales told by a newspaper reporter. In "Respectability," we meet Wash Williams, another victim of the femme fatale of American naturalism:

> Wash Williams was a man of courage. A thing had happened to him that made him hate life, and he hated it whole-heartedly, with the abandon of a poet. First of all, he hated women. "Bitches," he called them. His feeling toward men was somewhat different. He pitied them. "Does not every man let his life be managed for him by some bitch or another?" he asked. (122)

We later learn that Wash had been happily married to a beautiful woman until he discovered that the woman he loved had several other lovers and had been fooling him all along. Upon learning that he has been fooled, Wash sends his wife away to her mother's household. A few months pass and her mother asks him to come back. Upon his arrival, his wife, following her mother's advice walks in naked. Wash Williams strikes the mother and leaves. The femme fatale is responsible for the present degraded state in which Wash Williams finds himself.

Ernest Hemingway's *The Sun Also Rises* deals with a number of expatriates who suffer from the physical and psychological wounds of war. Lady Brett Ashley and Jake Barnes are two characters that best exemplify the effects war can have on an individual. However, as her only means of escape, Lady Brett Ashley takes pleasure in entrapping men and consequently breaking their hearts. She is a daring, dominating, manipulative woman who subverts even the most masculine man in the novel, Romero the bull-fighter. Although the novel deals primarily with what Hemingway terms "The Lost Generation," the novel also depicts another femme fatale who turns herself from victim to victimizer in a world that has compelled her to do so.

Nella Larsen's other novella, *Passing*, presents yet another example of a femme fatale. Clare Kendry, the protagonist, is suffering from her interracial blood the same way in which Helga Crane is suffering from the color of her skin. Yearning for acceptance and assimilation into the white culture, Clare chooses to pass as a white person. In her refusal to let heredity and environment control her, Clare has to pay a price. Thus, Clare suffers the pangs of ridding herself of her hereditary traits and concealing the truth about her racial background, and, at the same time, she suffers the pangs of her surrounding environment by pretending to be white. Amidst all of Clare's confusion and lies, Clare is able to victimize and manipulate the men around, including her Irene's husband. Eventually, Clare loses the battle and loses her life as well.

Katherine Anne Porter's "Old Mortality" depicts another femme fatale who is responsible for the destruction of men as well as the destruction of herself. Aunt Amy, who "was a spirited-looking young woman, with dark, curly hair cropped and parted on the side, a short oval face with straight eyebrows, and a large curved mouth" (173), is responsible for the gradual downfall of Gabriel and his subsequent death. After Amy repeatedly refuses Gabriel's proposals, she suddenly agrees to marry him. The marriage lasts for six weeks only and then Amy dies. Gabriel remarries but is driven to a life infused with alcoholism that brings him to his death. The femme fatale in this story has had fatal effects on her own life as well as Gabriel's.

Written serially in 1866 and published in 1975, Louisa May Alcott's *Behind a Mask: Or, A Woman's Power*, deals with a devious, shrewd, and destructive woman that goes by the name of Jean Muir. In the story, Jean Muir disguises herself as a governess and works for the Coventry family. Motivated by greed and the desire to acquire wealth, Jean Muir cleverly outwits the family she is working with and makes every man in the household fall in love with her. During the course of the events that take place at the Coventry estate, Jean Muir participates in a tableau vivant and takes roles as a murderess, a lover, and a queen, all of which are roles infused with power. Jean Muir is another example of a powerful femme fatale figure in American naturalism as she uses her charm and distinctive beauty to escape her low social status and poor background (she is an actress and has been divorced). Towards the end of the novel, Jean Muir successfully fools everyone around her, especially Sir John Coventry, to whom she gets married.

By providing examples of other femmes fatales in the literary tradition of American naturalism, this book emphasizes the fact that the femme fatale of American naturalism is distinct from the New Woman who was created at the turn of the twentieth century. The femme fatale is characterized above all by her effect upon men: A femme cannot be fatale if a man is not present in her life, even if her fatalism is eventually directed toward herself. Therefore, we witness McTeague, Hurstwood, Robert Lebrun, Dr. Anderson, Theron Ware, Jake Barnes, Sir John Coventry, Wash Williams, Gabriel, and many other male characters all suffering from becoming involved with the femme fatale of American naturalism. We also witness the negative and often deadly results of the femme fatale's actions on herself.

The New Woman, in contrast, comes to refer to a distinctive type of woman emerging from the changing social and economic conditions of the late nineteenth century. The New Woman is one who not only challenges the dominant sexual morality but who also begins to enter new areas of employment and education. While the New Woman is often threatening to the patriarchal world, she does not carry the sexual fatalism that the femme fatale of American naturalism carries. In Sarah Orne Jewett's *A Country Doctor*, Nan Prince provides a good example of the New Woman who is strong and courageous. Nan Prince rejects the traditional roles and conventional values ascribed for women at the time and attempts to realize an alternative social vision. She does not, like the femme fatale, use her sexuality to escape the moral and social conventions. What she does utilize, however, is her intellectual capabilities as she aspires to become a medical doctor. George Gerry falls in love with Nan and offers to marry her, but Nan rejects his offer because she wants to enter the medical profession and make a future for herself. Neither Nan nor George suffers from the consequences of her decision. Thus, the New Woman does not have the negative ramifications on herself or on the men she encounters as the femme fatale of American naturalism does. *A Country Doctor* ends with a victorious declaration of independence for the New Woman who has been able to finally make her own choices and follow her own aspirations. Nan

Prince looks up to the sky and says, "Oh God...I thank thee for my future" (351).

The central point of this book is to pinpoint the paradoxes inherent in each of these women in American naturalism who are simultaneously determined and free, malignant and benign, victimizers and victims, predators and prey. These paradoxes, along with the effects of heredity and environment, give birth to the femme fatale. This study has proven that the image of the femme fatale is one of great complexity and ambivalence. On the one hand, these women are troubled, perplexed, and helpless; on the other, they are insouciant, careless, and merciless. Consequently, the femme fatale is formed through her refusal to let heredity and environment take control of her. The juxtaposition of the good and the bad is present in each of the women discussed in this study.

Focusing on the female protagonists' use of their sexuality, my analysis aims to prove that the woman who was created by the American naturalists is not feeble and is not wholly defeated by heredity and environment. She struggles against the conditioning forces of her life and is consequently molded into a femme fatale. The depiction of the femme fatale has been a useful tool for the writers to show women trying desperately and diligently to fight back. It does not seem that the writers of this particular movement created this femme fatale figure with the intention of voicing a moral perspective against this figure. They do not stress the dangers of being a femme fatale as much as they stress the weaknesses and, paradoxically, the strengths of these women. Despite the fact that these femmes fatales are all eventually defeated, these writers are concerned with the social milieu that has caused the defeat more than the defeat itself.

Therefore, this book does not seek to stress the threats of being a femme fatale; nor does the book imply that the novelists who are creating this femme fatale figure are moralistic and are showing the dangers that the femme fatale poses to herself, the men she encounters, and society at large. However, this book aims to emphasize the social milieu and/or the hereditary traits that have shaped the femme fatale figure. In Trina's case, heredity serves as the dominating factor, whereas in Carrie's and Edna's cases, the focus of the writer shifts toward the social milieu that has given birth to the femme fatale. In Helga's situation, both heredity and environment act as the catalysts that shape her into a femme fatale.

By looking at the internal motivation for becoming a femme fatale of each of the women discussed in this book, the naturalistic writers focus on the inherited traits, the social construction, the social limitations, the confinement, the exploitation, and the patriarchal dominance that cause the woman to emerge as a femme fatale figure. The women created in naturalistic texts question and fight back against these social restrictions and confinements. Trina hopes to find a better life by marrying McTeague and struggles to rid herself of the ancestral blood running in her veins. Carrie retaliates against the capitalist exploitation and finds herself easily convinced by Drouet to choose a different path than working at the factory. Edna is confined in her marriage and seeks freedom from the constricting rules and regulations of the oppressive patriarchal world. She looks for individuality and her own space and freedom. Helga, on the other hand, is free of patriarchal oppression but is oppressed in a different form. She desires to be free, like Edna, but her sense of freedom is constricted because of the color of her skin. Helga exemplifies the dilemma of the mulatto character in American society, and as a result of being a mulatta, Helga drifts from place to place, searching for a place she can call home. All of the women discussed in this book are confined in one sense or the other, and we witness all of them struggling to break free from their individual cases of confinement.

Alas, the endeavors of these women eventually prove to be hopeless and fruitless. Trina is killed by McTeague, Edna commits suicide, Carrie realizes the emptiness of the successful life that she achieves, and Helga finds herself entrapped in childbirth and the cycle of life. None of these women achieve victory against the naturalistic world by becoming a femme fatale. Society will not change because of the actions of these particular women. The naturalistic world will not change either and will continue to deny women their free will and individuality. The image of Helga giving birth to one child after another at the end of the novel best exemplifies the fact that the naturalistic world is in full force. Helga is giving birth to more and more individuals who will struggle in this deterministic world the way she and many other individuals have struggled.

The fact that the naturalistic writers do in fact present a portrait of the femme fatale may result in a denunciation of this figure. However, to condemn the femme fatale means to overlook all the circumstances that compel her to become one. None of the protagonists in this study is portrayed as evil, and none of them intends to bring about destruction. They are merely fighting against heredity and environment. The amalgamation of vice and virtue is present in each of the women discussed here. Among the vices that are persistent in the novels are the protagonists' exploitation of their sexuality, their unwillingness to help their male counterparts, and their lack of pity. Among the virtues perhaps the first is strength, which may be seen as a moral quality in itself; it implies the courage to be strong in spite of social restraints. A second virtue is naturalness, that is, the quality of acting in accordance with one's nature and physical attractiveness. A third virtue is tolerance, especially of failure, frustration, and victimization.

I conclude this book by quoting Malcolm Cowley:

> The effect of naturalism as a doctrine is to subtract from literature the whole notion of human responsibility. "Not men" is its constant echo. If naturalistic stories had tragic endings, these were not to be explained by human wills in conflict with each other or with fate; they were the blind results of conditions, forces, physical laws, or nature herself. (65)

However, by examining the conditions that have created the femme fatale figure of American naturalism, human will is a persistent factor in each one of the women discussed in this book. Unfortunately, the human wills of Trina, Carrie, Edna, and Helga were not strong enough to conquer the "conditions, forces, physical laws, or nature herself," which Cowley mentions.

PRIMARY BIBLIOGRAPHY

Alcott, Louisa May. *Behind a Mask: The Unknown Thrillers of Louisa May Alcott*. Ed. Madeline Stern. 1866. New York: William Morrow, 1975.

Anderson, Sherwood. *Winesburg, Ohio*. 1919. New York: Viking, 1960.

Chopin, Kate. *The Awakening and Selected Stories*. 1899. Ed. Sandra M. Gilbert. New York: Penguin, 1984.

Crane, Stephen. *Maggie: A Girl of the Streets and Other Tales of New York*. 1893. New York: Penguin, 2000. 3–86.

Dreiser, Theodore. *Sister Carrie*. 1900. New York: Signet, 1961.

Fredrick, Harold. *The Damnation of Theron Ware*. 1896. Chicago: Herbert, 1896.

Gilman, Charlotte Perkins. *Women and Economics*. 1898. Ed. Carl N. Negler. New York: Harper & Row, 1966.

Hemingway, Ernest. *The Sun Also Rises*. 1926. New York: Scribner, 1954.

Howells, William Dean. *The Rise of Silas Lapham*. 1885. Boston: Riverside, 1957.

Jewett, Sarah Orne. *A Country Doctor.* 1884. New York: New American Library, 1986.

Keats, John. "La Belle Dame Sans Merci." *The Poems of John Keats*. Ed. Jack Stillinger. Cambridge, MA: Harvard University Press, 1978.

Larsen, Nella. *Quicksand and Passing*. Ed. Deborah E. McDowell. New Brunswick: Rutgers University Press, 1986.

Norris, Frank. *McTeague*. 1899. New York, Signet, 1964.

Porter, Katherine Anne. "Old Mortality." *The Collected Stories of Katherine Anne Porter.* New York: Harcourt, 1965.

Tarkington, Booth. *Alice Adams*. New York: Grosset & Dunlap, 1921.

Wharton, Edith. *The House of Mirth*. 1905. New York: C. Scribner's Sons, 1975.

SECONDARY BIBLIOGRAPHY

Ahnebrink, Lars. *The Beginnings of Naturalism in American Fiction.* New York: Russell and Russell, 1961.

Arms, George. "Kate Chopin's *The Awakening* in the Perspective of Her Literary Career." *Essays on American Literature in Honor of Jay B. Hubbel.* Durham, NC: Duke University Press, 1967. 215–228.

Bade, Patrick. *Femme Fatale: Images of Evil and Fascinating Women.* New York: Mayflower, 1979.

Berzon, Judith. *Neither White Nor Black: The Mulatto Character in American Fiction.* New York: Oxford University Press, 1978.

Black, Martha Fodask. "The Quintessence of Chopin." *Kate Chopin Reconsidered: Beyond the Bayou.* Ed. Lynda S. Boren and Sara de Saussure Davis. Baton Rouge: Louisiana State University Press, 1992. 95–116.

Cady, Edwin H. *The Light of Common Day: Realism in American Fiction.* Bloomington: Indiana University Press, 1971.

Clement, Priscilla Ferguson. "The City and the Child." *American Childhood: A Research Guide and Historical Handbook.* Ed. Joseph M. Hawes and N. Ray Hiner. Westport, CT: Greenwood Press, 1985. 230–255.

Cohen, Ronald D. "Child-Saving and Progressivism." *American Childhood: A Research Guide and Historical Handbook.* Ed. Joseph M Hawes, and N. Ray Hiner. Westport, CT: Greenwood Press, 1985. 268–290.

Cohn, Jan. "Women as Superfluous Characters in American Realism and Naturalism." *Studies in American Fiction* 1 (1973): 154–162.

Conder, John J. *Naturalism in American Fiction: The Classic Phase*. Lexington: University Press of Kentucky, 1984.

Cowley, Malcolm. "Naturalism in American Literature." *American Naturalism*. Ed. Harold Bloom. Philadelphia: Chelsea, 2004. 49–80.

Culley, Margaret, ed. *Kate Chopin: The Awakening*. New York: Norton, 1976.

Dillingham, William B. *Frank Norris: Instinct and Art*. Boston: Houghton Mifflin, 1962.

"Doings in New York: New York Society." *Godey's Lady's Book and Magazine* March 1887: 281–324.

Dyer, Joyce. The Awakening: *A Novel of Beginnings*. New York: Twayne, 1993.

Farrell, Edward. *The Femme Fatale Myth: Sources and Manifestation in Selected Visual Media 1880–1920*. Diss. School of Emory University, 1983.

Fleissner, Jennifer L. *Women, Compulsion, Modernity: The Moment of American Naturalism*. Chicago: University of Chicago Press, 2004.

French, Warren. *Frank Norris*. New York: Twayne, 1962.

Frohock, W. M. *Theodore Dreiser*. Minneapolis: University of Minnesota Press, 1972.

Fryer, Judith. *The Faces of Eve: Women in the Nineteenth-Century American Novel*. New York: Oxford University Press, 1976.

Gelfant, Blanche H. "What More Can Carrie Want? Naturalistic Ways of Consuming Women." *The Cambridge Companion to American Realism and Naturalism*. Ed. Donald Pizer. Cambridge: Cambridge University Press, 1999. 178–210.

Gerber, Philip. *Theodore Dreiser Revisited*. New York, Twayne, 1992.

The Grolier International Dictionary. 10th ed., 1981.

Harris, Susan K. *Nineteenth-Century American Women's Novels: Interpretive Strategies*. Cambridge: Cambridge University Press, 1990.

Hochman, Barbara. "Loss, Habit, Obsession: The Governing Dynamic of *McTeague*." *Studies in American Fiction* 14.2 (1986): 179–190.

Hussman, Lawrence E., Jr. *Dreiser and His Fiction: A Twentieth-Century Quest*. Philadelphia: University of Pennsylvania Press, 1983.

Larson, Charles R. *Invisible Darkness: Jean Toomer and Nella Larsen*. Iowa City: University of Iowa Press, 1993.

Lehan, Richard. *Theodore Dreiser: His World and His Novels*. Carbondale: Southern Illinois University Press, 1969.

Loeb, Lori Anne. *Consuming Angels: Advertising and Victorian Women*. New York: Oxford University Press, 1994.

Lundquist, James. *Theodore Dreiser*. New York: Ungar Publishing, 1974.

Marchand, Ernest. *Frank Norris: A Study*. New York: Octagon, 1942.

Martin, Wendy, ed. *New Essays on* The Awakening. Cambridge, UK: Cambridge University Press, 1988.

McAleer, John J. *Theodore Dreiser: An Introduction and Inter-pretation.* New York: Holt-Rinehart-Winston, 1986.

McDowell, Deborah, ed. *Quicksand and Passing by Nella Larsen.* New Brunswick: Rutgers University Press, 1986.

McElrath, Joseph, Jr. *Frank Norris Revisted.* New York: Twayne, 1992.

Miller, Ericka M. *The Other Reconstruction: Where Violence and Womanhood Meet in the Writings of Wells-Bernett, Grimke, and Larsen.* New York: Garland, 2000.

Mitchell, Clark Lee. *Determined Fictions: American Literary Naturalism.* New York: Columbia University Press, 1989.

Pizer, Donald. "Contemporary American Literary Naturalism." *American Naturalism.* Ed. Harold Bloom. Philadelphia: Chelsea, 2004. 255–270.

———. "Late Nineteenth-Century American Naturalism." *American Naturalism.* Ed. Harold Bloom. Philadelphia: Chelsea, 2004. 81–96.

———. *The Novels of Frank Norris.* New York: Haskell, 1973.

———. *The Novels of Theodore Dreiser: A Critical Study.* Minneapolis: University of Minnesota Press, 1976.

———. *Twentieth-Century American Naturalism: An Interpretation.* Carbondale: Southern Illionois Press, 1982.

Reedy, William Marion. "*Sister Carrie*: A Strangely Strong Novel in a Queer Milieu." *Critical Essays on Theodore Dreiser.* Ed. Donald Pizer. Boston: Hall, 1981. 157–159.

Reuter, Edward. *The Mulatto in the United States.* New York: Negro University Press, 1969.

Riggio, Thomas P. "Carrie's Blues." *New Essays on Sister Carrie.* Ed. Donald Pizer. New York: Cambridge University Press, 1991. 23–42.

Ringe, Donald A. "Romantic Imagery in Kate Chopin's *The Awakening.*" *American Literature* 43 (1972): 588–597.

Seyersted, Per. *Kate Chopin: A Critical Biography.* Baton Rouge: Louisiana State University Press, 1992.

Showalter, Elaine. "Feminist Criticism in the Wilderness." *The New Feminist Criticism: Essays on Women, Literature, and Theory.* Ed. Elaine Showalter. New York: Pantheon, 1985. 243–270.

———. "Tradition and the Female Talent: *The Awakening* as a Solitary Book." *New Essays on* The Awakening. Ed. Wendy Martin. Cambridge: Cambridge University Press, 1988. 33–58.

Sloane, David E. E. *Theodore Dreiser's Sociological Tragedy.* New York: Twayne, 1992.

Smith-Rosenburg, Carroll. *Disorderly Conduct: Visions of Gender in Victorian America.* New York: Oxford University Press, 1985.

Sollers, Werner. *Neither White Nor Black: Yet Both.* New York: Oxford University Press, 1997.

Thorp, Willard. *American Writing in the Twentieth Century.* Cambridge, MA: Harvard University Press, 1960.

Trasko, Mary. *Daring Do's: A History of Extraordinary Hair.* Paris: Flammarion, 1994.

Walker, Nancy, ed. *Kate Chopin: The Awakening: Complete, Authoritative Text With Biographical, Historical, and Cultural Contexts, Critical History, and Contemporary Critical Perspectives.* Boston: Bedford/St. Martin's, 2000.

Wall, Cheryl A. "Feminist or Naturalist: The Social Context of Kate Chopin's *The Awakening*." *Southern Quarterly* 17.2 (1979): 95–103.

———. *Women of the Harlem Renaissance*. Bloomington: Indiana University Press, 1995.

Wolkenfeld, Suzanne. "Edna's Suicide: The Problem of the One and the Many." *The Awakening*. Ed. Margo Culley. New York: Norton, 1976.

Ziff, Larzer. *The American 1890s: Life and Times of a Lost Generation*. New York: Viking Press, 1966.

INDEX

CPSIA information can be obtained at www.ICGtesting.com
Printed in the USA
BVOW042301090512

289838BV00002B/1/P